Perfect

SARDINIA

Travel with
Insider Tips

MARCO ⊕ POLO

Contents

For chapters: See inside front cover

TOP 10

Not to be missed!

**Our TOP 10 hits – from the absolute No. 1 to No. 10 –
help you plan your tour of the most important sights.**

⭐ **GOLFO DI OROSEI** ➤ 90

An unforgettable example of the wonders of nature: a boat trip to the staggeringly beautiful Gulf of Orosei, with its dream beaches, steep cliffs, grottoes and caves, is a must (photo on the left).

⭐ **QUARTIERE DI CASTELLO, CAGLIARI** ➤ 50

The capital's historical centre is not only an ambassador of the country's art and culture but also of the diversity of Sardinian cuisine. A highlight is the Castello district with the cathedral and the *Citadella dei Musei*.

⭐ **CAPO CÁCCIA & GROTTA DI NETTUNO** ➤ 108

A rocky promontory that rises majestically from the sea, home to the spectacular dripstone cave Grotta di Nettuno.

⭐ **NURAGHE SU NURAXI** ➤ 52

This mighty Stone Age bastion is one of the most impressive stone edifices dating back to the Nuraghic period.

⭐ **ARCIPÉLAGO DE LA MADDALENA** ➤ 130

A boat trip through the marine national park and around the numerous little islets and islands with their wonderful beaches is an unforgettable experience.

⭐ **VILLASIMÍUS** ➤ 54

The lively little town is surrounded by a rich marine environment and a magnificent coast with dozens of breathtakingly beautiful beaches.

⭐ **PENISOLA DEL SINIS** ➤ 72

The secluded peninsula surrounded by a lagoon teeming with fish attracts visitors with its unique rice grain beaches, the ancient Roman town of Tharros and its renowned fish restaurants.

⭐ **ALGHERO** ➤ 110

The harbour town is an architectural gem and also the starting point for trips to Capo Cáccia and the Grotta di Nettuno.

⭐ **SÁSSARI** ➤ 112

An authentic university town with oodles of culture; the lovely winding streets in the Old Town are ideal for strolling, shopping and lapping up the Mediterranean lifestyle.

⭐ **TISCALI VILLAGGIO NURAGICO** ➤ 92

A trip here is a real experience! The safe haven of Sardinia's ancient Nuraghic civilization was in a wide crater in the Supramonte mountains.

THAT
SARDINIA

Find out what makes Sardinia tick, experience its unique flair – just like the Sardinians themselves.

EVENING STROLL TO BASTIONE SAN REMY

When the heat of the day slowly abates and the setting sun glows across the Golfo degli Ángeli, the "Gulf of Angels", the inhabitants of the capital and its visitors flock to the "balcony" of Cagliari, to the Bastion of Saint Remy. You can see people strolling around the plaza, playing with their grandchildren, sitting flirting on the walls or enjoying the refreshing evening breeze over an *aperitivo* at a bar.

FEAST FOR THE SENSES

The Sardinians call the scent of aromatic herbs which the warm air wafts under the noses of visitors at the entrance to Ólbia harbour "*Il profumo di pastori*", literally "the perfume of shepherds". Along the coast and in the mountains, the fragrance is everywhere. That also applies for the "sound of Sardinia", the gentle jingling of the little bells of the flocks of sheep and goats. Do as they do in Sardinia: lie down and enjoy a wonderful picnic in their midst.

FAIRY HOUSES & GIANTS' TOMBS

Sardinia is an ancient island. Nowhere else in Europe has as many prehistoric sites. The most visible evidence of this is seen in the innumerable nuraghi, the towers named after the mysterious Nuraghic civilization who built them. You can discover many undeveloped giants' tombs, fairy houses, holy wells, temples and cult sites. No one can deny the magic and mystical aura surrounding these places.

BEACH LIFE ON LA CINTA

A beach paradise set against a spectacular backdrop. The Spiaggia de La Cinta is a beach paradise between a crystal-clear sea and white sand speckled pink by the flamingos. Rising majestically in front of it like a monster from the waves is the Tavolara massif. Here you can meet, swim and surf, or try your hand at paragliding. The cool and inviting beach bars serve ice-cold cocktails.

FEELING

Splashing and swimming in the crystal-clear water on the La Cinta beach

That Sardinia Feeling

CELEBRATING IN THE OPEN AIR

Regardless of whether it is the sheep-shearing period, harvest time or the village saint's special day, the Sardinians can always find a reason to have a celebration. These traditional festivities offer wonderful opportunities to become acquainted with the soul of the Sardinians, their hospitality, their cuisine and cultural traditions. Make sure you attend one of the many local events celebrated together with everyone in the community. Guests are always welcome!

THE WILDLY ROMANTIC MOUNTAINSCAPE OF BARBAGIA

Barbagia from its wildest and prettiest side! Anyone who loves walking as a way to unwind will find plenty

Sardinia offers pleasure for the eyes and the palate – here swordfish carpaccio

of great opportunities in the Foresta di Montes by Orgosolo. A narrow road leads to Pratobello and ends at the entrance to the wildly romantic mountain area at a forestry station. It takes just a good half an hour to reach the 1316 m (4,318ft) high peak of Monte Novo. The panoramic view from the top is sensational.

PANE, PECORINO & PORCHEDDU

It is best to wear your belt a little looser on Sardinia; the island is a mecca for those who love good food and good wine. Each region and village has its own specialities and wines. Thus a drive over the island becomes a gastronomic discovery tour. On the coast, you can find excellent seafood, in the mountains the traditional farmhouse fare. Regardless of whether you dine in the garden of the legendary country hotel Su Gologone on the sea terrace of the famous La Gritta in Palau near Oliena, or in the well-known Sa Muvara in Aritzo well-known for its mountain food, chances are it will be an epicurean and unforgettable evening.

LA DOLCE FAR NIENTE ON THE PIAZZA

Mediterranean lifestyle only needs a piazza and a mild summer night. One place right out of a picture book is the Piazza Centrale in the heart of the Old Town of Orosei. Sooner or later everyone sits down on a little wall or in a bar to indulge in *dolce far niente*, a very pleasant form of idleness.

The Magazine

A Small Continent
in the Mediterranean

Cast away in the middle of the Mediterranean, the Italian island of Sardinia seems more like a small continent. The second largest island after Sicily, Sardinia has a coastline of almost 2,000km (1,240mi) indented by tiny coves and guarded by towering cliffs.

Sardinia's Soul

Inland you will find a traditional land of shepherds, with stretches of sometimes impassable highland, criss-crossed with ravines, riddled with caves and covered in bristly scrubland – a place where it's very easy to forget that the sea is never far away.

Sardinia is different from other islands. Its inhabitants regard the sea as something barbarian, synonymous with those who came to plunder, *"furat chi beit dae su mare"* ("he who comes from the sea comes to rob"). The "robbers" included among others the Phoenicians, Romans, Arabs, Catalans, Genoese and Venetians. The Sardinians retreated from the

Cannonau vineyard near Jerzu

THE SARDINIAN LANGUAGE

The Sardinian language is a Romance language, Latin-based, but also revealing Spanish, Catalan, Corsican, Genoese and Arab influences. In addition, traces dating back to the Nuraghic civilization can also be distinguished. Besides Italian, over 80% of the islanders speak Sard. Owing to the isolated location of the mountain villages, very different dialects have developed. The main dialects are Logudorese (North and Central Sardinian), Nuraghic (Central and East Sardinia) and Campidanese (South Sardinia). Since 1999, the Sardinian language has been a recognised minority language.

coastline under foreign occupation to the impenetrable highland in the middle of the island, where they were never subjugated and thus able to uphold their ancient traditions. This is the key to understanding the Sardinian soul. Sardinians are shepherds and farmers, not fishermen and seamen. They fear the ocean and even see the Italians as those people *dal Continente*.

Freedom through Independence

Language, national cuisine, music, poetry or dance: there is no other island in Europe that upholds its traditions with the same devotion as the Sardinians. It is thanks to this knowledge passed down through the generations that the Sardinians have been able to retain their identity and independence. Every village has its own national dress, choir, handicrafts and specialities. Even today, the island is not dependent on tourism, instead producing a large percentage of what it needs through farming. It exports worldwide, products including for example the popular Pecorino cheese.

Through-and-Through Sardinians Don't Go to the Beach

Sardinians: Their character is marked by their pastoralist history. They have a deep love of the countryside, wine, dance and song; their deep faith is mirrored in the religious festivals and processions. Horses are their passion.

Anyone wishing to discover the real Sardinia, such as the traditional folk dance Ballu Tundu, danced in a circle to the shrill sound of a shepherd's pipe, the *launeddas*, has to go inland, away from the coast and up into the mountains of Barbagia. Only those who experience this will really appreciate the power and magic of this culture and the attraction of Sardinia as a holiday destination.

NURAGHI

Giants' Tombs and Fairy Houses

The more than 7,000 round stone towers rising up to 14m (45ft) above the landscape would be interesting from any era, but when you realise that these were built between the 12th and 15th centuries BC, they become mind-boggling.

Feat of Engineering

Nuraghi are built of huge stones that form walls and ceilings for as many as three interior floors. Built without mortar or any bonding substance, these walls have highly sophisticated inner staircases spiralling within their 2m (6ft) thickness. How prehistoric people engineered these constructions remains a mystery.

Just as puzzling is their purpose and use. Archaeologists have found no evidence that they were used as living quarters, such as fires, food or household artefacts. Many nuraghi were surrounded by villages of stone round huts, but with wood and reed roofs instead of the stone tholos domes of the Nuraghic towers. These reveal ample evidence of household use, so it is surmised that the towers

BUILDING THE NURAGHI

When the towers were built about 3,500 years ago, the true dome, using a keystone, had not been invented. Nuraghic builders used instead an ancient method called a tholos dome to roof each level. With this method, each succeeding course of stone overhangs inward from the last until they meet at the top.

A higher storey was added by laying a flat capstone over the top and filling in the edges to create a level floor.

were built for observation, defence and as symbols of power to warn off potential invaders.

Whatever their purpose nuraghi are among the most interesting and amazing prehistoric relics in the world, and they are widespread enough that visitors to any part of the island can find one close by to explore.

Supernatural Homes

It's easy to see how, millennia later, people came to view the mysterious graves left by their prehistoric forebears as supernatural places. Earth mound coverings of chambered tombs washed away and revealed what indeed look like tombs for giants (*tombe dei giganti*), while little "rooms" carved into soft ledges and cliffs would make credible homes for wee folk (*domus de janas*, "fairy houses"). Archaeologists have identified over a thousand such group burial sites, and what little they know of the builders is gleaned from the bronze, pottery and stone offerings left with the deceased. Holy wells (*pozzi sacri*) – natural springs that were set up around the cult and ceremonial sites – add to the variety of prehistoric sites that pepper the island.

> "How prehistoric people engineered this construction is still a mystery"

You might think that seeing one of these prehistoric sites is enough, but they can become positively addictive. Each is a bit different, each reveals a little more – or adds to the puzzle of these ancient peoples. And each is interpreted in a different way, or left as it stands with no interpretation at all, places where 21st-century people can commune undisturbed with the ghosts of their ancient past.

Nuraghe Losa (opposite); Nuraghe Su Nuraxi (below left); Nuraghe Santu Antine (right)

LIFE'S A **BEACH**

Sardinia has Italy's most beautiful coastline and some of the world's most idyllic beaches. Kilometres of blonde sands dip into aquamarine and emerald green waters. Elsewhere, tiny coves and picturesque harbours beg to be explored.

For many the Costa Smeralda (➤ 134) – Emerald Coast – is the reason that Sardinia is famous. In the 1950s, while yachting in the northeast of the island, the fabulously wealthy Prince Karim Aga Khan IV and his chums became spellbound by the translucent emerald-green waters and romantic little coves. He found a group of businessmen to join him in developing it as a resort that would protect its natural beauty, and so the Costa Smeralda was born. Those jewel-like colours take on every hue from sapphire blue to sparkling turquoise, so dazzling in contrast with the sugar-white sands that you can't help but don your Prada shades. And yet, this is only a tiny area of the island's magnificent wealth of beaches.

Secret Coves
Great swathes of the Sardinian coast remain uninhabited, with pines, juniper and prickly pears encircling occasional sandy beaches, sea and granite rocks – just as the Costa Smeralda once was. In all directions, each area

The turquoise waters of La Cinta near San Teodoro contrast with its white-sand beach

of coast has its own gems. Some are reached only by little paths surrounded by junipers, pine trees, oleander and eucalyptus, others by boat.

Superb Beaches

On the west coast, dunes soar and surfers carve their creamy wakes, while at the island's northwestern point white sands shelve from Ísola Asinara into the most brilliant turquoise sea. The pretty northeastern resorts of Palau, Santa Teresa di Gallura, Báia Sardinia and Cannigione might lack the glamour and exclusivity of the Costa Smeralda but many prefer their laid-back feel, and all have beautiful beaches, such as the romantically gorgeous Valle della Luna. On the central-eastern coast, by the Gennargentu National Park where the vast limestone massif of the Supramonte plummets almost vertically into the Gulf of Orosei, you will find the highest and most awesome cliffs in the entire Mediterranean area. This paradisiacal bathing area can only be reached by boat. In the south, emerald-cobalt water laps pinkish-white sand in the Báia Chia, the "Pearl of the South".

Crowded or Secluded?

All of Sardinia's beaches are open to everyone. While it may be absurd to suggest that anyone could ever tire of the land that gave us Verdi, Vesuvius and Versace, those mainland Italians who want a change of scenery for their summer breaks come to Sardinia in their droves. Yet, even in August at the height of the holiday season, only the main town beaches get crowded. While many visitors prefer the privacy and space of the quiet coves farther away from the beach car park, Italians like to parade up and down on the more sociable town beaches.

CARNIVAL &
other Festivals

The island frequently bursts into life for its festivals. Music fills the air along with the aromas of sweets, bread, herbs and cheeses. If you feel it tugging at your wilder instincts, don't be surprised: Sardinia was born out of rugged traditions.

The biggest festivals are usually religious in origin, but others celebrate annual occasions such as the harvest, the turning of the seasons or an historic event. *Carnevale* (literally "farewell to meat"), usually celebrated in February, sees masked characters, such as the *mamuthones* of Mamoiada (➤ 97) in the Barbagia, enacting battles between devils and animals. In picturesque little Bosa (➤ 120), the *Carnevale* celebrations have lusty, if not blatantly open, sexual connotations.

The island's biggest festival is the religious *Sagra di Sant'Efisio* in Cagliari. On 1 May the patron saint's image is carried on a cart drawn by decorated oxen from the capital to Nora, where Sant'Efisio was executed. It returns on the night of 4 May accompanied by throngs of people dressed in traditional costume and by the music of the *launeddas*. Unique to Sardinia, this woodwind instrument consists of three reed pipes, two with finger holes and one drone, and is played by musicians using their cheeks as a "wind bag". Their sound accompanies many festivals.

Sássari: Cavalcata and Candelieri

The second city, Sássari (➤ 112), has two major festivals. On the penultimate Sunday in May, the *Cavalcata Sarda* parade (➤ 44), hundreds of Sardinians in traditional costumes celebrating a victory over the Saracens in AD1000. Afternoon horse races through the streets are followed by evening dancing and merrymaking. On 14 August, the night before the Assumption,

From left to right: Young women in colourful national costume; Sant'Efisio Procession through Cagliari; riders during the *Cavalcata Sarda*; a toddler in traditional dress

nine mammoth *candelieri* (candlesticks), weighing up to 300kg (47 stone), are carried in a large procession from the *gremi* (city guilds) through the town in honour of the Virgin Mary. The festivities date back to the 16th century and a solemn promise made by the inhabitants when the plague was raging in Sássari.

Núoro and San Salvatore

In late August the mountainous interior celebrates with a colourful parade in Núoro (➤ 94) for the *Sagra del Redentore* (Christ the Redeemer; ➤ 44, 96). After several days of parades, music, dancing and fireworks, the festival culminates in a procession to the statue of Il Redentore on Monte Ortobene. In September, the *Festa di San Salvatore* is celebrated by young men running barefoot from Cabras to San Salvatore (➤ 78).

Gastronomic Festivals

There are many food festivals as local delicacies come into season. Among others, the sea urchin festival takes place in Alghero (➤ 110) in January, the *Sagra dell'Agrume* (Citrus Festival) in Muravera, north of Villasimíus, and the *Sagra delle Castagne* (Feast of Chestnuts) fills the streets of Aritzo in the Gennargentu mountains in October.

SARDINIA'S
OTHER ISLANDS

Caught between Africa and Europe, equidistant between the Italian and North African mainlands, Sardinia was well described by the writer D H Lawrence (1885–1930) as being "lost between Europe and Africa and belonging to nowhere". However, Sardinia is not just one island, it is a whole group clustered around the main one.

Somewhat smaller than Sicily, Sardinia is the second largest island in the Mediterranean, measuring 257km (160mi) long by 109km (68mi) wide. Surrounding it are offshore islands, each with its own special characteristics and even history.

In the southwest, Ísola di Sant' Antíoco (►60) is Italy's fourth largest island, after Sicily, Sardinia and Elba. Linked by a Roman causeway to the mainland, it was the original site of the Phoenician city Sulci founded in the eighth century BC. While this island's charms are in its abundant prehistoric and early Christian sites, the nearby smaller Ísola di San Pietro (►60) oozes charm of a more recent origin.

Although the Sardinians have no strong tradition as fishermen, the islanders of San Pietro are descended from Genoese coral fishermen (*tabarchini*), who came from the Tunisian islet of Tabarca in 1738. A version of Genoese is still spoken in this very picturesque little "piece of Liguria". Named after St Peter, who supposedly took shelter during a storm here on his way to Cagliari, the island is renowned for its excellent fish, especially tuna.

Sunset at Palau on the Costa Smeralda

Donkeys and Goats

Other islands take their name from animals, such as Ísola Asinara ("Donkey Island"; ➤ 116). Lying in the northwest opposite Cape Falcone, the island is uninhabited but has a population of some 250 miniature albino donkeys (pictured below). Now part of a national park, it's possible to visit by guided boat excursions only. You may not get to see the little donkeys, but look out for other inhabitants, including falcons, pigs, mouflons and goats.

Ísola Caprera, on the other hand, is named after goats, and is part of the Maddalena Archipelago (➤ 130), a cluster of 40 islets and seven main islands off the north coast. Caprera is home not only to goats but also to kestrels, green pines and wild orchids, and to Giuseppe Garibaldi, the national hero of Italian unification in the 19th century, whose former home here is a museum. From La Maddalena, the main island, there are boat trips to inlets and jaw-droppingly beautiful beaches in the archipelago.

King of the Island

There is even an island with its own king. Beyond Ólbia and the Costa Smeralda the knife edge of the island of Tavolara (➤ 133) rises 564m (1,850ft) sharply from the sea.

The monarchy was founded in 1836 when King Carlo Alberto gave the rock to its sole inhabitant, the fisherman Giusseppe Bertoleoni, thereafter known as the "King of Tavolara". His descendants still keep court at Restaurant Da Tonino. Tavolara has about a dozen inhabitants, all from the Bertoleoni family. Tavolara is a restricted military area, in which the Americans conceal nuclear submarines.

The **Wild** West

Sardinians are among Italy's finest riders, especially in the "Wild West" of Oristano province. They often ride pure-blooded Arab steeds and show off their skills at breakneck speed in spectacular festivals. You can enjoy horse riding and trekking at one of the many equestrian centres.

Sa Sartiglia

One of Sardinia's liveliest equestrian festivals is held in Oristano (➤ 74). Since 1200, it has always taken place on the last Sunday and Monday before Lent. The town erupts into a frenzy of colourful costumes and thundering hooves over the two-day event. Its origins go back to tournaments, when knights on their galloping steeds had to put their lances through a ring suspended from a rope. Masked, costumed riders gallop towards a six-pointed star hanging from a rope and try to pierce it with their swords. This is followed by a free-for-all, with daredevil feats of skill.

Masked riders perform daring feats on horseback during Sa Sartiglia in Oristano

S'Ardia

Between 6 and 7 July every year, the most daring and brave horsemen in the village of Sedilo take part in the wild and frantic *S'Ardia* (➤ 44). Three riders receive a yellow, a red and a white *pandela* (pennant), which mark them out as the representatives of Christianity. The first *pandela* gallops off without warning, the second and the third *pandela* have to prevent the leader being overtaken by any of the other "heathen" riders taking part in the race. Shouting crowds line the route and hundreds of riflemen shoot blank cartridges loaded with black dust. The horsemen circle the church six times. The race ends in the steep descent towards the narrow Victory Arch of Constantine. Horses bolt and the excitement of the crowd reaches a crescendo of deafening cheers but no one seems to worry. It is all part of the ritual that makes mainland Italy's *palio* races look like child's play. Sedilo is off the SS131 Abbasanta–Núoro road, a few kilometres from Abbasanta.

Horse-Riding Excursions

For forays of your own, Oristano is well equipped with riding excursions and courses. Ala Birdi, near Arboréa, has excellent riding facilities for all levels and ages (tel: 0783 80500; www.horsecountry.it).

Elsewhere on the island *agriturismo* farms and larger resorts offer riding to guests and to the public. In Aggius, in the Gallura mountains, Il Muto di Gallura (tel: 079 620 559; www.mutodigallura.com) maintains a stable of Arabian horses that guests can ride, and in the wild landscapes of Ísola Caprera, part of the nearby Arcipélago de la Maddalena, Cavallo Marsalla Centro Ippico (tel: 347 235 9064; www.lamaddalena.it/barabo.htm), has year-round guided horse-trekking trips.

Maneggio Li Nibari (tel: 348 335 0098; www.maneggiolinibari.it), north of Sassari in Stintino, offers horse-riding trips on Cape Falcone from June through October. Also around Abbasanta, Unicorn Trails (www.unicorntrails.com) organizes guided trips for six to eight riders on their Anglo-Arab-Sardinian thoroughbreds, exploring wild landscapes and beaches.

Top: Masked participants in Oristano's Sa Sartiglia

Right: The exciting S'Ardia race through the village of Sedilo

SARDINIA'S
Colourful Past

Even if you know nothing else of Sardinia's past, you may have heard of the mysterious Nuraghic towers that have puzzled archaeologists and travellers for centuries. But that's only one layer of Sardinia's tumultuous history, and there are nearly 5,000 years of it waiting for you to discover.

That past extends back even farther if you browse through Sardinia's splendid museums, where you'll find stone objects created 10,000 years ago.

From this prehistoric period also come the many *domus de janus*, or "fairy houses" (► 13) – tombs cut into rock – and the megalithic burial chambers called "giants' tombs" (► 13). You'll find these burial sites around Arzachena (► 137, Costa Smeralda), at Sant'Andrea Priu (► 120) in the Valle dei Nuraghi (south of Sássari), at Necropoli di Anghelu Ruju (north of Alghero) and other sites across the island.

But you're more likely to head first for one of Sardinia's real blockbuster sights – the great stone Nuraghic towers (► 12) built between 1800BC and 500BC. The most complete and best interpreted of these are Nuraghe Su Nuraxi (► 52), Nuraghe Losa (► 76) and Nuraghe Santu Antine (► 117).

Geography doesn't make it practical to visit sights from each era in chronological order, but

The Romanesque Basilica della SS Trinità di Saccargia, Sássari

The ancient burial site of Tomba dei Giganti (Giants' Tomb), Li Lolghi

with a little basic knowledge of the progression of invaders, it's easy to put each in its place as you travel.

Early Visitors

Sardinia's first "invaders" came peacefully and seemed to be welcomed by the Nuraghic people. The Phoenicians arrived as traders and they established towns near the sea, around safe harbours at Nora (► 56), Tharros (► 73), Sulki and elsewhere. Those sites give you a feel for their cities and their intriguing *tophets* – burial places for children – marked by carved stones. See an outstanding collection of these on site at Sant' Antíoco, where there are also fascinating earlier necropoli caves.

Pugnacious Punics

The peaceful cultural and material exchange between the Sardinians and Phoenicians ended abruptly with the Punic invasion from Carthage late in the ninth century BC. Islanders joined forces with the Phoenicians, but were no match for the military-minded Carthaginians. Here began the Sardinians' turn inwards as they fled the coast for the security of the mountains. This was also the beginning of the realisation that *"furat chi beit dae su mare"* ("he who comes from the sea comes to rob"), which led to a greater emphasis on inland settlements.

But the Carthaginians couldn't sustain control in the face of a highly organized Roman empire on the move, and Sardinia became a colony of

GARIBALDI SLEPT HERE

Sardinia's role in Italy's Risorgimento – the mid-19th-century campaign that united various smaller kingdoms into one Italy – is mostly connected to its dynamic leader, Giuseppe Garibaldi (pictured right), considered the father of his country. He chose the island of Caprera for his home, and today Italians visit his modest villa as a national shrine.

Rome in 238BC. Locals retreated further into the wild Barbagia mountains to escape capture.

Roman Remains

The Romans made good use of the Phoenician cities at Tharros and Nora, expanding them and building their own on top of them. They built the first roads, connecting Cagliari and Sássari with what would become the route of the modern Carlo Felice highway. They built baths, which you can tour at the hot springs now known as Fordongiánus (▶ 80), and villas. They enlarged the mines that had drawn the Phoenicians here, and brought Christian prisoners to work them, unwittingly introducing Christianity. In the fourth and fifth centuries, the first Christians were martyred in Sardinia; some of their tombs can be seen in Sássari and Cagliari. Sardinia's only catacombs remain on Ísola di Sant' Antíoco (▶ 60).

> "The realisation was that 'he who comes from the sea comes to rob'"

When the centre of the Roman empire moved to Constantinople, Sardinia began its own Byzantine period, which lasted from the fifth to the tenth century, during which the Christian presence expanded and the first bishops were appointed. Little remains of this period, save a church in Cabras and San Saturnino in Cagliari. Government was delegated to four judges, the Giudicale.

Medieval Sardinia

At the beginning of the 11th century, Pisan and Genoese troops were sent to reclaim the island from Arabs, whose increasing raids had again forced locals into the interior. Throughout the early Middle Ages, Romanesque architecture flourished, as Christianity took hold and churches and monasteries were constructed. They range from modest little churches to the most outstanding example, SS Trinità di Saccargia (▶ 114), influenced by the Pisans, whose craftsmen followed the new governing force to the island.

A path leads up to Torre di Longosardo at Santa Teresa di Gallura

Then Came the Spanish

Italian domination ended in 1297, when Pope Boniface VIII presented the entire island to Jaime II, King of Aragon, beginning four centuries of Catalonian rule. He gave fiefdoms to 400 Catalan families to settle there, many of them around Alghero (➤ 110), where the Spanish influence still shows in both Gothic-inspired architecture and the language. Spanish watchtowers dot the coast of Sardinia, built to stave off pirate attacks.

In the early 1700s the island passed to the Piedmont Savoy dynasty, which sent Italian engineers and architects to strengthen fortifications and modernize its cities. Sardinia gradually became more Italian, as Cagliari's neoclassical Marina neighbourhood shows.

The 20th Century

World War II took a heavy toll on Sardinia, not only in lives lost in battle, but in the devastating bombing of Cagliari. You'll see reminders of that war along the north coast, where concrete bunkers remain of coastal defences. But a more outstanding site is the town of Carbonia, one of the few of Mussolini's planned cities that survives almost intact.

To see the later 20th century's impact, look no further than the pseudo-Aegean enclaves of the Costa Smeralda (➤ 134). Planned and built by the Aga Khan and his associates in the 1960s to create a millionaire's paradise for their own slice of the *dolce vita*, this coast was the darling of the jet set, and became the model for other purpose-built resort towns.

Sardinian Cuisine

"Sardinian cooking is of a poor nature. It is the cooking of the farmers and shepherds. Sardinian cooking may be poor in some ways but is extremely rich in others, for example it has flavour, intelligence, versatility and an exotic nature."

So writes Raffaele Balzano in *Sardegna a Tavola*, a Sardinian cookery book. He might also have added that Sardinia is organic or free range in virtually everything it produces and that many of the delicious flavours come from the wild herbs that carpet the rich pastureland.

Just as significant is the fact that locally grown ingredients are not a trendy new idea here – they are integral to Sardinian food culture, and are almost taken for granted. That's not surprising when you remember that Sardinians have always looked to their own land for sustenance and have never relied heavily on imports.

You'll notice the absence of foreign and ethnic eating places, too; restaurants have to survive after the tourist season, and Sardinians prefer Sardinian food. Updated and tweaked maybe, and attractively presented, but true to the local ingredients and traditions. That's not to say that new chefs have not created quite a buzz with stylish new dishes and innovative interpretations of old favourites. Restaurants such as Cagliari's Dr Ampex

Wine grapes for fine Sardinian wine; local cheeses on a market stall; spitted pork in Su Gologone

(➤ 64) and Alghero's Villa Las Tronas (➤ 121) embrace the Sardinian food culture in new and interesting ways, updating it without losing the real essence. And others such as Tenuta Pilastru (➤ 140) in the mountains above the Costa Smeralda are presenting typical local dishes in stylish and up-market settings.

Traditional Cooking
Meat forms the basis of traditional Sardinian cuisine, *la cucina tipica Sarda:* lamb, beef, kid goat and wild boar are spit-roasted or grilled with fragrant herbs. A national dish is suckling pig *(porceddu)*, which sometimes you must order a day ahead to allow time to massage the skin of the piglet in herbs, olive oil and sea salt before slow-roasting over an open fire, then serving on a bed of fragrant myrtle leaves. You will see other popular menu offerings that are not to everyone's taste: *sa córdula* (roasted or barbecued sheep's entrails), *sa tratalia* – goat stuffed with bacon – or lamb intestine or *piedini e testini d'agnello* – a dish of cooked lamb's head and trotters. Other favourites include horse and donkey meat. You will only find *bue rosso* beef (from the island's resilient russet-red breed of cow) in the Monte Ferru region.

Crisp Bread
Although not found in all restaurants, the traditional (and delicious) Sardinian bread is *pane carasau*, which was already being baked 1000BC. A particularly delicious kind is *pane guttiau* – baked with salt and olive oil, and sprinkled with rosemary.

Pasta Sardinian-style
Like everything else on the menu, pasta takes on its own forms in Sardinia. *Fregola* is like pearls of toasted couscous, served in soup or *con arselle* (with

clams). *Malloreddus* are small ridged gnocchi-like pasta, prepared with a light tomato sauce and often sausage bits. *Culurgiones* are similar to ravioli, but filled with potato and cheese seasoned with local herbs. A real delicacy is *spaghetti alla bottarga*, made with mullet roe, which are dried and grated over the freshly cooked pasta mixed with olive oil. *Bottarga* is known as "Sardinian caviar" – delicious and expensive.

Seafood

Although Sardinians are *pastori, non pescatori* – shepherds, not fishermen –

LONG LIFE AND HAPPINESS

The traditional Sard greeting *A Kent'Annos* ("May you live to 100") is no mere jest. Sardinia has the world's highest percentage of people past their 100th birthday; around 135 people per million live to celebrate it, while the Western average is nearer 75. Sardinians credit the fresh local food and red wine for their longevity.

seafood is widely available. Lobster *(aragosta)* is a great favourite, as well as *calamari* (squid), *polpo* (octopus) or *ricci di mare* (sea urchins).

Pecorino Rules

Cheese-making is an art form on Sardinia and the delicious pecorino made from ewe's milk accounts for more than three-quarters of Italy's *pecorino romano*. Many different varieties of Pecorino are available all over the island: as cream cheese *dolce sardo*, young as a medium hard cheese *medio* or as *staggionato*, a parmesan-style Pecorino, which is at least 12 months old. Sardinian Pecorino specialities are, for instance, spicy and piquant *fiore sardo*, the production of which is exclusively restricted to the island, or the notorious *casu marzu*, in which live fly maggots (that you eat with the cheese) turn the cheese into a soft spreadable mass. For a sweet cheese experience, try *sebada*, like a doughnut, oozing with ricotta cheese and thick, creamy mountain honey.

Fine Wines

Sardinian wines are among the world's finest, but so prized and produced in such small quantities that vintages often run out quickly. They are therefore not widely exported, so enjoy them while you can in Sardinia. The most well-known red wines are made from the Cannonau (Grenache) grape or the Monica grape; for whites look for Vermentino and Vernaccia. The Cannonau is one

> "Meat forms the basis of traditional Sardinian cuisine"

of the oldest vines in the world; there is evidence of its cultivation in 1200BC. The red wine pressed from the grapes is the ultimate Sardinian red wine.

The most exclusive wines produced on the island, in the meantime of international acclaim, are mainly the red wines pressed from the Carignano grape "Turriga" from Argiolas in Serdiana and "Terre Brune" from Cantina di Santadi as well as the white "Capichera", a refined Vermentino from Tenuta Capichera near Arzachena. Well-known dessert wines are "Moscato" and the prized "Vernaccia" from Oristano and Bosa.

Sardinia's favourite liqueur *mirto rosso* is produced from the myrtle berry, the slightly lightly variety *mirto bianco* from the shrub's flower. *Bresca dorada* ("golden honeycomb") is regarded as the premium label and is made using honey and not sugar.

Firewater

The island's strong drink, distilled from the winemaking leftovers, rather like grappa, is known as *su fil'e ferru* – "rod of iron". Locals say that it's named after the practice of marking its hiding place with a piece of wire, but, at around 40 per cent proof, it could also have something to do with the drink's head-splitting strength.

Opposite: *Pane carasau* **is the local crispy bread; café terraces on Via Roma in Cagliari**

A Natural
PARADISE

Shepherds lean on their crooks under the shade of juniper trees watching their flocks graze the aromatic *macchia* vegetation. Eagles nest in the wave-sculpted granite cliffs and wild boar take cover in the forests of cork and holm oak. By the golden dunes, carpets of vivid magenta mesembryanthemums, nick-named *buon giorno* flowers, open their daisy-like petals to greet the sun.

Everywhere you go you'll hear the tinkling bells of sheep and goats. There are many unique species on this isolated island, such as the mouflon – long-horned wild sheep that are on the brink of extinction on mainland Italy. Giara di Gesturi is home to the *cavallini* – miniature wild horses – and the island of Asinara (► 116) is famous for its little albino donkeys. If you're very lucky, you might spot a *cervo sardo* (Sardinian deer) roaming in the Gennargentu mountains (► 98, 152). The World Wildlife Fund has established the Monte Arcosu Nature Reserve in the Sulcis mountains in the southwest to protect indigenous deer and wild boar.

Birdlife
Home to 200 different bird species – a third of the entire number found in Europe – Sardinia attracts many of them with the rich pickings of succulent shrimps in the lagoons. Some like it so much that they have changed their migratory habits, such as the colonies of pink flamingos that now nest and breed in Cagliari's lagoons. Endemic to Sardinia are rare birds such as the golden eagle, peregrine falcon and Eleonora's falcon. It's the last place in Europe where the latter are found, and their numbers are increasing

UNDER THE WATER
The sea teems with marine flora and fauna, and a highlight is the rich, red coral around the coast of Alghero (► 110). Divers prize the north coast from the Gulf of Arzachena to the Gulf of Asinara for its fish-filled reefs. Dolphins are often sighted off Alghero) and around the Maddalena islands (► 130).

Left to right: Flamingos; Wild horses; *macchia mediterranea* at Capo Cáccia

dramatically. On the coast road from Alghero to Bosa you may spot some of Italy's largest colony of the endangered griffon vulture. Anyone wishing to catch sight of these giants of the air, which can have a wing span of up to 3m (10ft), should stop off at the car park by Capo Marargiu. Around 100 of these birds nest in the inaccessible cliffs.

Fragrant Flora

All year, but especially in spring and autumn, the island is ablaze with flowers. Roses and thick carpets of brilliantly coloured *buon giorno* flowers are intertwined with exotic orchids, hibiscus, oleander and swathes of bougainvillea. A thick carpet of *macchia mediterranea* (Mediterranean maquis) covers most of the land in a tangled and fragrant profusion of lavender, rosemary, wild fennel, juniper and myrtle.

Wild Landscapes

Constant winds have sculpted the northeast's rocky landscape into bizarre and otherworldly shapes, especially on Capo Testa, and at the Valle della Luna (Valley of the Moon, ➤ 138) near Aggius. In Parco Nazionale de Golfo di Orosei (➤ 90), which protects the pristine southeastern coast and the island's highest peaks, the 2.5km (4mi) long Gola Su Gorruppu canyon (➤ 98) is one of Europe's deepest at 426m (1,400ft). Caves, including the breathtaking Grotta di Nettuno (➤ 108) or the Grotta Su Marmuri at Ulassai, carve into the cliffs that guard the island's shore.

Island
ARTISTRY

Haute-couture fashions created from cork, entire towns offering open-air canvases for artists, a mountain village known worldwide for its exquisitely handcrafted knives (*Sa Resol*) – the arts are alive and well in Sardinia.

The island's dynamic artistic tradition dates back to the extraordinary bronze work by Nuraghic peoples, and in the same way that today's chefs are experimenting with new interpretations of the Sardinian cuisine, today's artists draw their inspiration from the materials, techniques and even designs of their ancestors, but express them in new ways.

There's a lot to stimulate ideas. The stunning bronze and gold work in the Museo Archeológico Nazionale (▶51) in Cagliari shows off Sardinia's long legacy of metalwork. Knives are legendary, the most famous and desirable of them forged by blacksmiths in Santu Lussúrgiu (▶79), north of Oristano. Handles are carved of local horn or olive wood. While the knife-makers hold close to original styles and designs, artists elsewhere use these as a starting point for their own creative spirit. But they still favour the native materials prized here for centuries – coarse wool from Sardinian sheep, wood from the chestnut forests, cork and local plants for baskets.

Even today there is a strong heritage of localized crafts, with certain towns noted for particular products. This is certainly true of the highly prized wool carpets sought by collectors, who still travel to the little stone town of Ággius (▶138) high in the mountains near the Costa Smeralda. Woven by hand, much as they have been for centuries, their unique texture is formed by tight loops that stand above the surface, often in contrast to the background. Motifs and colours range from very traditional to striking contemporary designs. The techniques may be old, but the artistry is strictly from the 21st century.

Left to right: bronze figures; detail from a mural in Orgosolo; a choice of different handicrafts; mural in Orgosolo

SHOPPING FOR SARDINIAN ARTS

Sardinian styles and techniques are constantly evolving, which makes shopping for local arts especially exciting. To see the finest in all traditions, from ancient arts to cutting-edge design, seek out one of the ISOLA galleries (➤43), located in Cagliari (➤66), Núoro (➤101) and Oristano (➤84).

In other arts, as in rug-making, there is a strong reliance on Sardinian motifs and materials for inspiration, but only as a starting point. Artists and designers continue to create and innovate. In Témpio Pausánia (➤138), a town surrounded by cork oak forests, designer Anna Grindi has developed a cork fibre comparable with silk for its lightness and delicacy. Her high-fashion clothes have been acclaimed since they first appeared in 2000.

Not all Sardinia's arts are tactile. The tradition of painted towns began in the late 1960s when artist Pinuccio Sciola began creating murals in San Sperate, near Cagliari. Other Italian and international artists followed, and today San Sperate's streets are decorated by hundreds of these, representing every artistic style. Better known are the political satire murals in Orgosolo (➤97), a remote village high in the Supramonte mountains: What once started as a rebellion against the severe poverty and the occupation by the military of the highland pastures *pratobello* that were essential for the existence of the village animals, has become an internationally renowned open-air gallery in which every style and theme has found its niche.

Timeless Motifs

Nearly a century ago, D H Lawrence described the brightly coloured designs woven into wool saddlebags. The traditional motifs he saw can be traced back many centuries, yet he would recognize those same inspirations today. They may be interpreted in different ways, but in equally brilliant shades, the crimson poppy foremost among them. Animal designs, especially deer and mouflon that are also used in the traditional masks of the mountain village festivals, are echoed in sleek lines in contemporary metal sculpture.

Weaving local patterns into a carpet in Muravera

Finding Your Feet

First Two Hours

Arriving by Air

You have three options if you are flying to Sardinia. Cagliari, the international airport serving the capital of Sardinia, is the gateway to the southern coast. It is 8km (5mi) northwest of the city centre. Alghero airport is located 10km (6mi) to the north of the town in the Northwest and national flights from the Italian mainland fly here, predominantly via the island connection from Milan and Rome. Ryanair also offers flights to Alghero. The airport from Ólbia, 5km (3mi) southeast of the city centre is the goal of international scheduled and charter flights: Machines from Milan, Rome and Verona as well as Easyjet, AirBerlin and TUIfly fly here.

Ólbia Airport

- The airport at Ólbia, grandly called Aeroporto Ólbia Costa Smeralda (tel: 0789 563 444; www.geasar.com), is served by international and charter flights as well as flights from Milan, Rome and Verona. easyJet operates regular flights here. The airport is 5km (3mi) southeast of the centre.
- **Car rental desks** lie within easy walking distance of the main arrivals terminal. Look for the sign "Terminal Autonoleggi".
- Take the SS125 **directly into Ólbia** (roadworks are a constant hazard in this city, so there are usually diversions). If travelling to the **Costa Smeralda** take the SS125 from the airport to join the SS131.
- The stop for the **city buses** is located on the right of the exit from the arrivals hall. City buses 2 and 10 run to Ólbia Centre (Station) every 20 minutes between 6:15am and 11:45pm; journey time about 10 minutes. Tickets are available on board (€1.50) or from the ticket machine in the terminal (€1). Information: tel: 800 91847 (toll free).
- The **taxi rank** is in front of the arrivals terminal. An average fare into Ólbia is €20.

Cagliari's Airport

- Cagliari's airport is called **Élmas** (www.sogaer.it).
- The airport is 6km (4mi) northwest of the city centre.
- **Car rental desks** and parking are just outside the terminal; exit the arrivals hall to the right, following signs for Autonoleggi/Rent-a-Car, to a series of small kiosks across the access road, and look for your car rental company's logo.
- In the **centre of Cagliari**, follow the broad, four-lane Viale Elmas, which will take you – like the E27 which runs practically parallel to it – directly to the Via Roma. Anyone travelling southwest/towards Iglesias, takes the Viale Elmas in the opposite direction (Decimomannu).
- The **Elmas Aeroporto station** provides a connection between the airport and the centre. It can be reached from the departures hall and several escalators. The trains take five to seven minutes to reach the main station at Piazza Matteotti. Tickets cost €1.25. The arrival and departure point for all trains to and from Cagliari at the airport is next door. There is thus a direct connection to the regional express trains to Oristano, Macomer, Ólbia and Sássari. The bus connections to Cagliari have been stopped.
- At the exits on both the ground floor and first floor there are several **taxi companies**. A taxi into Cagliari costs about €25 (tel: 070 400 101).

Alghero's Airport

- Alghero's airport is called **Fertilia** (tel: 079 977 128; www.aeroportodi alghero.it). There is a tourist information office in the arrivals terminal (tel: 079 977 128; open daily).
- Alghero's airport is served by many domestic airlines servicing mainland Italy, mainly to and from Milan and Rome. Ryanair also has frequent flights here. It is in the northwest of the island and is 10km (6mi) north of Alghero.
- **Car rental desks** are inside the arrivals terminal, and rental cars are parked outside in the car park opposite the main exit to the airport.
- For **Alghero centre**, take the SP44 south, then the SS127, which flows into the SP42 just in front of the town, which in turn leads directly to the car park at the harbour in front of the Old Town. Distance 12km (7.5mi), duration about 20 min.
- The stop for the bus to Alghero is about 150m to the right of the exit of the arrivals hall. The airport shuttles of **ARST** (Linie AI.F.A.) run between 5:20am and 11pm every hour to Via Cagliari, right by the Old Town and harbour. The journey takes about 30 minutes. Tickets are available on board (€1.50) or from the ticket machine in the terminal (€1).
- You will find **taxis** outside the exit gates of the arrivals terminal. Taxis into the centre of Alghero cost about €20. There is a 24-hour switchboard (tel: 079 975 396 or 079 989 2028).

Arriving by Sea

- There are many car and passenger ferry companies **from mainland Italy** to Sardinia. The most important connections are the stretches from Genoa and Livorno to Ólbia and Golfo Aranci. The shortest crossing is from Civitavecchia (near Rome) to Ólbia/Golfo Aranci. Off season, the timetable is very meagre; some stretches are not even covered. During the high season (July/Aug), it is best to book in good time.
- There are **direct routes** from Marseille in France and, sometimes, from Toulon.
- There are many **links from Corsica** to Sardinia, the most regular of which is from Bonifacio to Santa Teresa di Gallura.
- For **more information** on all Mediterranean ferry companies, visit www. traghettiweb.it; www.holidays-in-sardinia.com or www.aferry.co.uk

Tourist Information Offices

- **Sardinia:** Assessorato del turismo, Viale Trieste 105, 09123 Cagliari; tel: 070 606 7005; www.sardegnaturismo.it, sardegnaturismo@regione.sardegna.it
- **Cagliari:** Assessorato Turismo, Via Cadello 9/b, 09121 Cagliari; tel: 070 409 2962, Info-Tel. 800 203 541, turismo.provincia.cagliari.it
- **Carbonia-Iglesias:** Via Mazzini 39, 09013 Carbonia; tel: 0781 67261; www.sulcisiglesiente.eu
- **Medio Campidano:** Via Carlo Felice 267, 09025 Sanluri; tel: 070 935 6700; www.provincia.mediocampidano.it
- **Ólbia-Tempio:** Via Nanni 39, 07026 Ólbia; tel: 0789 557 600; www.olbiatempioturismo.it
- **Oristano:** Piazza Eleonora 18, 09170 Oristano; tel: 0783 368 3210; www.provincia.or.it; www.gooristano.com
- **Sássari:** Piazza d'Italia 31, 07100 Sássari; tel: 079 206 9000; www.provincia.sassari.it
- **Núoro:** Piazza Italia 7, 08100 Núoro; tel: 0784 238 878; www.provincia.nuoro.gov.it

Getting Around

The ideal way to get the most out of Sardinia is by car, but it is also possible to see most of the island's highlights by bus and by train – that can take a bit of time. Cars can be rented from all three airports (▶ 36) or in most main cities and larger towns. Be aware that many of the seaside resorts are pedestrianized in the evenings in summer.

Driving

- You need a valid **full driver's licence** and, if not a member of the EU, an international driving permit.
- **Contact your insurance company** before departure to ensure you are covered outside your home country.
- If you bring in a **foreign-registered car** you must also carry the vehicle's registration. The Green insurance card is not obligatory, but practical, because it simplifies things in the case of an accident.
- To **rent a car** on the island you must be over 21 and have a full valid driver's licence which is at least a year old. It is necessary to make a deposit, and it is very difficult to obtain a rental car without a credit card. It is often cheaper to rent a car when you book your holiday as part of a "fly-drive" package. Cars can also be booked through the central telephone numbers or websites of the major rental companies in your country of origin or via internet portals, such as www.holidayautos. com or www.autoeurope.com before leaving.

Driving Essentials

- **Drive on the right** and overtake on the left. Give way to traffic from the right unless otherwise indicated.
- It is Italian law to use your **headlights** outside built-up areas at all times (including daytime).
- If a driver **flashes his headlights**, it means he's coming through, not that he's conceding you right of way.
- There are no tolls on Sardinia. On the main highways and on secondary roads the **speed limit** is 90kph (56mph), in built-up areas 50kph (30mph).
- The **main north-south road**, which is mostly dual carriageway, is the SS131 Carlo Felice highway, which runs the length of the country from Cagliari to Sássari and on to Porto Tórres. Turning off from the SS131 is the SS131bis, which takes you to Ólbia via Núoro.
- Other SS *(superstrada)* roads are the SS130 running west from the Carlo Felice to Iglésias, and the new dual carriageway that takes you from Sássari part of the way to Alghero. New motorways are available on the south coast between Villasimius and Cagliari as well as on the east coast from Arbatax to the Costa Rei/Villasimius.
- Many of Sardinia's **secondary roads** are very scenic but also very twisty with plenty of hairpin bends. The *strade bianche* (white roads) are often unpaved and little more than rough tracks, more suitable for off-road vehicles than those with a low axle. Be aware that should you have a puncture or flat tyre, you will have to replace it at your own cost.
- **Petrol** is *benzina*, unleaded petrol is *senza piombo*, diesel is *gasolio*. Fuel stations are spaced at relatively regular intervals along the SS roads, but most close at lunchtime and after 7:30pm. However, many are self-service and take credit cards and euro notes (which must be in good condition and not dog-eared).

- **Parking** can be a nightmare in the big centres. Blue parking spaces are subject to a charge, white parking spaces are free of charge, yellow spaces are reserved for buses and taxis. Black and yellow striped curbstones indicate that parking is not allowed! You pay at meters in cities, or a parking attendant will issue you with a ticket. Average rates are €0.50 per hour.
- **Adhere to the traffic rules!** The fines in Italy are very high (penalties can be between €39–€311!) and there are a lot of checks.
- If your **car breaks down**, you are only allowed to get out of the car when you have put on the safety vest! You must have the safety vest inside the vehicle (not in the boot). Switch on the hazard warning lights and place the red warning triangle about 50m behind your vehicle and call 116.
- If you are **involved in an accident** put out the red warning triangle and call the police (tel: 112/113) and/or ambulance (tel: 118). Do not admit liability or make potentially incriminating statements. Ask witnesses to remain on the scene, exchange names, addresses and insurance details.

Buses

- Sardinia has a **good network of buses** which link not only villages and towns but also beaches (although these only operate during the summer).
- The **blue buses of ARST** (Azienda Regionale Sarda Trasporti; tel: 800 865 042 toll free; www.arst.sardegna.it) are the backbone of the public transport system on the island. ARST provides connections to practically every place on the island. In addition, there are numerous other bus services offering local connections as well as island-wide express bus routes. Be warned: private bus lines do not depart from the central ARST bus stations, but have their own stops (express buses: www.gruppoturmotravel.com).

Ferries

- There are regular **ferries from Palau to the island of La Maddalena** (all year around the clock) operated by: Saremar (tel: 199 118 877; www.saremar.it), EneRmaR (tel: 0789 708 484; www.enermar.it) and Delcomar (www.delcomar.it;tel: 0781 857 123).
- Enermar also operates regular sailings from **Portovesme to Ísola di San Pietro's Carloforte** (from about 5am to 8pm; duration about 35 min.). In the summer, the ferries from Delcomar sail around the clock. Also running between the **islands of San Pietro and Sant'Antíoco** (Carloforte–Calasetta, duration about 20 min.) are ferries from Enermar and Delcomar.
- There are also frequent services between Santa Teresa di Gallura and Bonifacio on **Corsica** operated by Saremar and by Moby Lines (tel: 199 303 040; www.moby.it; duration about 20 min.).

Trains

- The **train network** is fairly limited. There is only one FS (Ferrovie dello Stato) line operating between Golfo Aranci/Ólbia to Cagliari with branches off to Sássari, Iglesias and Carbonia (tel: 892 021 from a land line or 12 892 021 from a mobile phone; www.trenitalia.com).
- Besides that, there is a light railway service that is now managed by ARST, offering year-round and seasonal connections. The tourist train *trenino verde* (little green train) runs between various destinations during the season (tel: 070 343 112 or toll free 800 460 220; www.trenino verde.com). However, the operator ARST has announced that it will be stopping all of its light rail services in 2016.
- **Validate your ticket** when entering the station by punching it in one of the machines on the platform.

Accommodation

Sardinia offers a large choice of accommodation, especially on the coast – whereby rooms in the north and east are on average more expensive than in the south and west. Some good B&Bs are on offer, and rural accommodation in *agriturismi* is widely available. As the season is short in the resorts (often June to September) early booking is recommended.

Hotels

- **All hotels are graded** from one star to five stars. The criteria for stars are usually based on the number, rather than the standard, of facilities.
- **"High season"** prices usually run from July to the beginning of September, the most expensive period being during the *altissima stagione*, the "high season", the two weeks around Ferragosto (15 August). During this time there may be minimum stays imposed upwards of three days and/or full board.
- The old *pensione* classification that used to refer to **a simple hotel** no longer exists, but you may still see one-star hotels calling themselves *pensione*. Usually these premises have shared bathrooms. Two-star hotels have private bathrooms, and rooms in three-star hotels usually have TV and telephone. Four-star properties have correspondingly more facilities and higher quality, while luxury five-stars offer every comfort – reflected in the price. There are several of these in Sardinia, mainly around the Costa Smeralda and nearby resorts, and on the coast near Cagliari. All accommodation prices are much lower out of high season.

Other Accommodation

- **B&Bs** have become increasingly popular and can be excellent value. The standard varies considerably and ranges from simply furnished rooms without a bathroom/WC to enchanting apartments with a terrace. It is thus well worth enquiring and having a look round in advance! For more information contact local tourist information offices or Bed & Breakfast Sardegna (www.bebsardegna.eu) or Sardegna B&B (www.sardegnabb.it).
- *Agriturismi* are usually countryside farmhouses or cottages, often with various activities on offer, such as horseback riding, trekking, biking and excursions to sights of interest. Food is the highlight here though, because the host families, who are involved either in farming or sheep-rearing, **serve home-cooked dinners** with locally grown produce, and the meals are almost always very lavish. For non-resident guests it is absolutely essential to book in advance. Information is available at www.agriturismo.it; www.agriturismodisardegna.it and www.terranostra.it.

Villas and Apartment Rentals

- Several companies offer self-catering in Sardinia, including: www.holidays-in-sardinia.com; www.interhome.com; www.rent-sardinia.com; www.justsardinia.co.uk; www.exploresardinia.it

---

Accommodation Prices

Expect to pay for a double room per night:

| € under €90 | €€ €90–€155 | €€€ €155–€250 | €€€€ over €250 |

Food and Drink

Food and drink is usually of a high standard in Sardinia and, in many places, is extremely good value. Whether you choose from *la terra* (land) or *il mare* (sea), there is plenty in the authentic Sardinian cuisine found throughout the island to satisfy even the most discerning gourmet.

Eating Places

■ Similar to mainland Italy, differences between the **various types of restaurant** are no longer so clearly defined. While a *ristorante* used to be an upmarket and expensive establishment and a trattoria was cheap and simple, the two have become increasingly blurred.

■ An *enoteca* is a wine bar that has a good selection of wines by the glass, accompanied by salamis, cheeses and a choice of snacks or light meals. You will also find the odd *birreria* where you can get a beer (or glass of wine) with snacks and light meals.

■ The *gelateria* – or ice-cream parlour – remains perennially popular, as with all Italian destinations committed to glorious *gelato*.

Eating Hours

■ Bars usually open around 7 for **breakfast** (*prima colazione*). A caffè (espresso) cappuccino and *cornetto* (croissant) is the usual Sard fare, which, incidentally, the locals almost never take sitting down.

■ By 1:30 many people are tucking into **lunch** *(pranzo)* and it can be a very leisurely affair. After all, everything stops for the siesta and businesses and shops close for up to four hours every afternoon.

■ **Dinner** *(cena)* is the family meal. It is customary to dress up when going to a *ristorante* (at the earliest from 8, but generally about 9–10). Casual clothing is inappropriate. Dogs are not welcome in restaurants.

Meals

■ A word in advance: it is an error to believe that you have to order a full-course meal. Even the Sards often only take individual courses. A **full-course meal** comprises antipasti, *primo piatto, secondo piatto* and a dessert.

■ **Antipasti**, meaning literally "before the meal". You will find featured on many menus both meat *(di terra)* and fish *(di mare)* options. Typical Sardinian antipasti are *di terra* and consist of *salsiccia* (Italian sausage), smoked meats, ham, lardo, pecorino, olives and *pane carasau*.

■ *Il primo* is the **first course**, usually pasta or soup *(suppa)*.

■ *Il secondo*, **the main course**, is meat or fish and seafood. The Sardinian speciality is *porcheddu*, the Sardinian variation of roast suckling pig, and lamb and boar.

■ *Dolci* (puddings) and **formaggi** (cheeses) are both Sardinian favourites. *Seadas are very popular*, dumplings filled with cream cheese and honey.

■ Meals can be followed by **coffee** – espresso is the Sard and Italian way (never cappuccino after dinner) – grappa or *mirto*, the local liqueur made from myrtle berries.

Vegetarians

■ Sards are meat eaters – and love crudities. Vegetarians will always find something in the traditional Sardinian cuisine, be it raw vegetables, tomatoes, cucumber, fennel or asparagus, salad, soups or pasta.

Finding Your Feet

A growing number of restaurants on the coast have now adapted to the needs of vegetarians.

■ Chicken *(pollo)* and ham *(prosciutto)*, let alone fish, are often **not considered to be proper meat**, so asking if a dish is vegetarian may result in a misleading answer; instead ask what's in it.

Sardinian Specialities

■ Baking the traditional bread, often known as *pane carasau* (➤ 27) is like a rite of passage in Sardinia. Deliciously light, crispy and thin, it is often referred to as "music bread", for it is supposed to be as flat as a sheet of music, *foglio da musica*.

■ Also unique to the island is **mullet *bottarga*** – delicate, amber-coloured roe known as "Sardinian caviar".

■ The lush, herb-scented pastureland is perfect for grazing animals, and produces tangy ***pecorino sardo* cheese** (➤ 29), a particular delicacy.

Drinks

■ **Sardinian wines** (➤ 29) are available almost everywhere and are generally good and inexpensive, especially if you opt for a carafe *(sfuso)* rather than a bottle. Sardinia is known for its **sweet dessert wines**, including Vernaccia, Moscato and Malvasia, as well as the heady red Cannonau.

■ As far as **spirits** go, Sardinia's version of grappa, *fil'e ferru* (➤ 29), is a fiery 40 per cent proof. *Mirto,* the Sardinian liqueur, is made from alcohol, myrtle berries and sugar.

■ **Beer** *(birra)* means lager in Italy. It's usually served in two sizes: *píccola* (small, 33cl) or *grande* (large, 66cl). If you ask for *birra nazionale* you'll get Italian Peroni or Sardinian Ichnusa, cheaper than imported brands.

Cafés and Bars

■ It's always less expensive to **stand at the bar** than sit at a table. You pay at a separate cash desk *(cassa)* for your order and then take your receipt to the bar and repeat your order.

■ Choosing to **sit at a table** means that the waiter will quickly take your order. What you shouldn't do is pay at the bar and then sit down with your drink.

Paying and Tipping

■ At the end of the meal ask for the **bill** *(il conto)*.

■ Almost everywhere you pay a **cover charge** *(pane e coperto)*, which is usually around €2 per person. **Service will also be added** in many restaurants, in which case you don't need to tip. If service is not included then 10 per cent would be an acceptable tip.

■ By law, the restaurateur is obliged to give you an **itemized receipt** *(una ricevuta fiscale)*, which you must take with you when you leave.

Dress Code

■ Italians in general tend to make more of an effort than foreign visitors. While most coastal areas are very relaxed, chic restaurants in cities such as Cagliari and Sássari **like guests to dress up**.

Restaurant Prices
Expect to pay per person for a meal, excluding drinks:

€ under €26	€€ €26–€55	€€€ over €55

Shopping

You will find crafts, ceramics, embroidered goods and tasty Sardinian morsels across the island. In cities you will also find good shops and a couple of department stores.

Craftware

There is a very rich tradition of craftware (➤ 32–34) on the island, but before heading off to the souvenir shops try to check out the authentic article in the ISOLA outlets. The Istituto Sardo Organizzazione Lavoro Artigiano (thankfully ISOLA for short), is responsible for taking care of and upholding the traditions of Sardinian craftsmanship and has outlets in places such as Cagliari, Núoro, Porto Cervo, Oristano, Alghero and, especially, Sássari, which has a big shop in the Giardini Púbblici (currently closed for renovation work). Here you will find a good range of handicrafts, each piece of which is authenticated.

Crafts

- **Ceramics** tend to be crafted in simple patterns and colours and you can find beautiful traditional pieces for everyday use in the Campidano region.
- For **cork** products, go to Sardinia's cork oak centre, the mountain town of Tempio Pausania and its surroundings.
- Filigree **gold and silver jewellery** is manufactured all over the island. Cagliari, Sássari, Dorgali and Bosa are particularly famous for it.
- **Carpets** and woven products made of *orbace*, untreated sheep's wool, are particularly attractive. Well-known producers can be found in Ággius, Mogoro and Samugheo.
- Bosa is famous for its *fileti di Bosa*, delicate **lace** and embroidery.
- Handcrafted Sardinian **shepherd's knives** make a very special souvenir. The best cutlers are located in Pattada, the "Sardinia's Toledo", in the mountain village of Santu Lussúrgiu (➤ 79) and in Guspini.
- Carnival masks from Barbagia, based on age-old models and made of wood, clay and leather, make a lovely memento. Only a few master craftsmen such as Signore Mameli in Mamoiada still produce them.

Food and Drink

For gourmet delights, Cannonau wine (increasingly believed to be the elixir of longevity), olive oil, pecorino cheese, *miele di corbezzolo* (the renowned Sardinian honey) and *torrone* nougat should all be high on the shopping list.

Entertainment

The island offers a plethora of entertainment from summer open-air festivals and concerts to opera, cutting-edge theatre and dance and pageants and festivities celebrating a prized local delicacy or saint's day. Nightlife throbs around the resorts and in the university towns such as Sássari and Cagliari.

Information

- The tourist offices in individual towns have comprehensive listings on local events. Also consult visitor centres for up-to-date details of local nightlife.

Finding Your Feet

Festivals

There are **festivals for every season** (➤ 16). Some celebrate the harvest, many are religious, others involve shows of equestrian expertise, and most are ancient in origin. But all are spectacular and a wonderful opportunity for dancing, feasting and immersing yourself in the infectious Sardinian love of life. A good overview of the many large and small *sagre, feste ed eventi tradizionali* on the island can be found at www.sagresardegna.it. The following are just a taster:

■ **Carnevale** (Carnival, Feb/March) is celebrated throughout the island but in very different ways. Whilst the customs and processions in Tempio Pausania and Bosa are fun, cheerful and frivolous events, the *carnevale* reflecting more Pre-Christian traditions in the Barbagia villages, seen in the primeval, gruesome masked characters, such as Mamuthones, Merdules and Maimones, have a more gloomy appeal.

■ **Sa Die de Sa Sardigna** (Sardinian Day, 28 April) commemorates the Vesper Insurrection *(vespri sardi)* of 1794 that led to the expulsion of the Piedmontese from Sardinia. The leaders' arrest is re-enacted in costume in the San Remy bastion, Cagliari, and musical shows go on late into the evening.

■ **Sant'Efisio** (1–4 May) is one of the island's most colourful festivals; it takes place in Cagliari in honour of Sardinia's patron saint (➤ 16, 66).

■ **Cavalcata Sarda,** Sássari (penultimate Sun in May) is a costumed pageant celebrating a victory over the Saracens in AD1000, followed by a spirited horseback gallop through the streets.

■ **S'Ardia,** Sedilo (6–8 July) is a spectacular but dangerous horse race between Oristano and Núoro (➤ 21).

■ **I Candelieri,** Sássari (14 Aug) sees giant timber "candles" paraded through the streets in the city's big feast (➤ 17, 112).

■ **Sagra del Redentore,** (➤ 13, 92) a procession in national dress through Núoro and up Monte Ortobene to the statue of the *redentore*, the Redeemer.

■ **Sagra di San Salvatore**, on the first Saturday in September, hundreds of barefoot men dressed in white carry the statue of San Salvatore about 7km (4.3mi) from the Santa Maria church in Cabras to the Chapel of San Salvatore on the Sinis peninsula and, on Sunday, return it to Santa Maria.

Sports

■ **Swimming** is good all around the coast.

■ **Windsurfing or kite-surfing** are popular everywhere, although the winds are especially good on the north coast. The west coast has some terrific surf at the beaches around Buggerru.

■ **Sailing** is the royal pastime – especially on the Costa Smeralda – where it is possible to rent a yacht if you haven't brought one with you.

■ **Snorkellers and divers** will find an underwater paradise in the limpid waters, and there are many schools and PADI-registered diving outfits scattered around the island.

■ For **golf enthusiasts** Sardinia has two of Europe's most beautiful 18-hole courses – Pevero Golf Club at the Costa Smeralda's Cala di Volpe and Is Molas Golf Hotel at Santa Margherita di Pula.

■ There is wonderful mountain terrain to be explored and **hiked** over, especially in the Gennargentu and Supramonte mountain ranges.

■ **Bolted rock climbing** is very popular around Cala Gonone.

■ **Horse trekking** (➤ 17) is very popular in the Barbagia region, and plenty of seaside resorts offer the opportunity to canter along the sands.

Cagliari & the South

 **Little Treats**

Cagliari's Balcony
Enjoy the view of the Old Town and Golfo degli Angeli from the **Bastione San Remy** (➤ 48).

Stroll Through the Fragrant Island
Walk along the narrow trail enveloped by the beguiling scents of the Mediterranean countryside to the wildly romantic **Capo Ferrato** (➤ 55).

Visit "Maestra del Bisso"
Go to the Museo del Bisso in Calasetta (Sant'Antíoco) to see the studio of the last woman to make **sea silk** (➤ 60).

Getting Your Bearings

Sardinia's capital Cagliari is a busy, salty port – the island's largest city by far – and a tantalizing pot pourri of ancient and modern. This southern part of the island was especially attractive to the Phoenicians and Romans, and the area is peppered with souvenirs of their stay. But the Nuraghic civilization was here, too, leaving behind their impressive fortress at Su Nuraxi. And then there are the beaches – some of the island's most beautiful – and all within striking distance of the city.

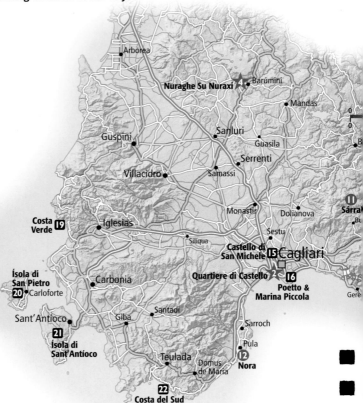

Getting Your Bearings

Known as *casteddu* (the castle) in the Sardinian language, Cagliari perches on top of a hill overlooking its beautiful gulf, the Bay of Angels. The sand-yellow city walls with their defensive tower and ochre-coloured houses once sent author D H Lawrence into raptures, as can be seen in his book *Sea and Sardinia*.

The Castello quarter is the Old Town and also home to the fascinating Museo Archeológico Nazionale. The lower town, or Marina quarter, is the perfect place for strolling and dining in the maze of little streets behind the Via Roma. In the west and east, the town is bordered by enormous *stagni*, shallow lagoon lakes and salt flats, the nesting ground of many different species of bird.

A little further inland is Marmilla, a rural area of extinct volcanoes and *giare*, table mountains, the home of wild horses even today. Looming up from the plains at the foot of the Giara di Gesturi plateau is the Nuraghic bastion Su Nuraxi. To the west the unspoilt Costa Verde offers a sight of incomparable beauty. Dozens of dream beaches can be found on the Costa del Sud and all around Villasimíus and the Capo Carbonara in the east.

Four Perfect Days

If you're not quite sure where to begin your travels, this itinerary recommends a practical and enjoyable four days exploring **Cagliari** and the south of the island, taking in some of the best places to see. For more information see the main entries (➤ 50–61).

Day 1

Morning
Travel to – or wake up in – Cagliari. Walk around ⭐ **Il Castello Quarter** (➤ 50). Enjoy a coffee at the Caffè delle Arti in der Via del Fossario, just a few steps away from the cathedral, and then visit the Museo Archeológico Nazionale (➤ 51).

Lunch
Have a picnic by **Bastione San Remy** or try for a table outside in the De Candia bar/restaurant (Via Marco de Candia 3, just by the Bastione).

Afternoon
Do as the locals do: take a trip to Cagliari's 10km (6.5mi) long beach **16 Poetto** (➤ 58). This spectacular beach and its bars are a must regardless of the weather.

Late afternoon and evening
Stroll around Cagliari and indulge in some retail therapy. Via Manno is good for fashion shops, while the department store Rinascente (open Sun) is on Via Roma, enjoy an aperitif under the arcades. Have dinner at **Dal Corsaro** or at **Da Serafino** (Marina quarter, ➤ 64).

Day 2

Morning
Take the SS131 north in the direction of Sanluri and then the SS197 northeast signposted Barúmini. ⭐ **Nuraghe Su Nuraxi** (➤ 52) is just outside it. Have a coffee in the bar across the road, then join a guided tour.

Lunch
Try Barúmini's **Sa Lolla Albergo Ristorante** (➤ 65). It serves delicious specialities from the Marmilla region.

Afternoon
Drive along the Giara di Gesturi (exits at Gesturi and·Tuili; ➤ 53) and take a walk to see the dramatic countryside and wild horses for yourself.

Day 3

Morning
Take the SS195 running along the **22 Costa del Sud** (left; ➤ 61) to Chia and relax on the beach.

Lunch
In Portoscuso, the ferries depart for Carloforte on the **20 Ísola di San Pietro** (➤ 60), famous for its tuna fish dishes. Recommendable is the **Da Nicolo** (➤ 65) run by Italy's nationwide star Luigi Pomata.

Afternoon
Stop in Pula and visit the archaeological site of **12 Nora** (➤ 56).

Day 4

Morning
Take the scenic coastal road to ⭐**Villasimíus** (➤ 54), wander through the little town and go for a swim at the beautiful beach of Porto Giunco.

Lunch
Now, it is worth stopping off at Castiadas to visit the museum in the old prison Le Vecchie Carceri. Then relax on a boat trip to **17 Ísola dei Cávoli** (➤ 58) and **18 Ísola Serpentara** (➤ 59).

Evening
Start the evening with an *aperitivo* on Piazza Gramsci in Villasimíus, before eating at **Carbonara** (➤ 64).

⭐Quartiere di Castello, Cagliari

Known as the *città d'acqua e di luce* – city of water and light – the Sardinian capital is a vibrant place. The first inhabitants settled here at the end of the third millennium BC and its monuments trace the island's history from its ancient origins to the present day. The Phoenicians called it Kàralis, meaning "rocky place", and when you look out from the dramatic ramparts over the limestone hills, this name seems very apt.

The historic centre within the bastioned walls is known as the Castello, or "Casteddu", as the locals refer to the whole city. It is compact and, although steep, is relatively easy to walk around. Defences were erected here by the Pisans after they took over the Byzantine city in 1217, though the present walls are Catalan and Piedmontese extensions. West of the Bastione San Remy, next to the university, the white 14th-century Pisan **Torre dell'Elefante** is one of the only two remaining towers. Look for the sculpted elephant at the base, and the portcullis, which was once festooned with the heads of executed prisoners. A climb to the top rewards with altogether more savoury views from the terrace.

In the centre of Castello is the **Cattedrale di Santa Maria**. It was originally built in the 13th century, but few vestiges of its former Gothic glory remain after rebuilding in the 17th century and a makeover for the 2000 Jubilee.

Cagliari's Castello invites you to wander round and explore

Quartiere di Castello, Cagliari

D H Lawrence commented that it had gone through "the mincing machine of the ages, and oozed out baroque and sausagey". However, there are still some treasures inside, including the two stone pulpits (originally one) on each side of the main doors, which were carved for Pisa cathedral in 1162 and presented by the Pisans to Cagliari in 1312.

Detail of the facade of the Cattedrale di Santa Maria

Cittadella dei Musei – Museo Archeológico Nazionale

Here you'll find the island's most important collection of artefacts from **prehistoric to Roman times**. Spanning three floors, the museum's first level is devoted to the pre-Nuraghic millennia, including obsidian tools and little round fertility stone goddesses – part of the Great Mother Goddess cult often found in "fairy houses" (➤ 13) – bronze statuettes used as votive offerings, and jewellery, from necklaces of fox teeth *(canini di volpe)* to an exquisite filigree gold necklace and earrings dating from the fourth century BC.

Largo Carlo Felice

This is Cagliari's most **important street**, where, in late spring and autumn, jacaranda trees put on a breathtaking display. At the southern end is Via Roma, lined with cafés, bars and elegant shops, and the place to watch the evening *passeggiata*.

Insider Tip

TAKING A BREAK

Have a drink or snack at the **Caffè degli Spiriti** (www.caffedeglispiriti.com) on the terrace at Bastione San Remy and admire the lovely views.

✚ 178 C2

Torre dell'Elefante
✉ Via Università
🕐 May–Sep daily 10–7; Oct–April 9–5 💶 €3

Cattedrale di Santa Maria
✉ Piazza Palazzo ☎ 070 663 837
🕐 June–Sep daily 8–8; Oct–May 8–noon, 4–8 💶 Free

Museo Archeológico Nazionale
✉ Piazza Arsenale ☎ 070 655 911
🕐 Tue–Sun 9–7:15 🚍 Circolare
💶 €5, combined ticket with Pinacoteca Nazionale (National Galery): €7

INSIDER INFO

Of the two towers, the **Torre dell'Elefante** is the better choice to climb, rather than the Torre San Pancrazio, as it has **access to the top terrace**.

Insider Tip

⭐4 Nuraghe Su Nuraxi

In Sardinian dialect, *su nuraxi* means simply "the nuraghi". This site is the finest and most complete Nuraghic complex on the island and is a UNESCO World Heritage Site. It looks like a beehive, surrounded by a honeycomb of the remains of buildings.

The complex at Barúmini, which was extended and reinforced in the first half of the first millennium BC under the Carthaginians, is the **finest and most complete example** of this remarkable form of prehistoric architecture. Visible for miles around, the main central tower of Su Nuraxi rises over a small plain, surrounded by other **nuraghi** to form a star-shaped system. Yet for centuries it was buried among the other hills. It wasn't until 1949 that excavation began, by the Sardinian archaeologist Giovanni Liulli, who became convinced that the hummock concealed Nuraghic treasures. It took six years to uncover it and excavations still continue today.

Exploring the Complex

Tours depart from the ticket office on the hour (duration one hour) in the company of a guide who is usually multilingual. You are **not allowed to walk on the site unaccompanied** as it is potentially quite dangerous. The terrain is very uneven and some scrambling up and down in confined spaces is necessary.

The oldest section is the huge **three-storey central tower** that was originally some 18m (60ft) high but now rises to 13.7m (45ft). It is estimated to date back to 1500BC and is thought to have been buried by the Sards during the time of the Roman conquest. What remains today is remarkably well preserved.

Built of dark basalt blocks, the central tower is believed to have been **constructed from volcanic stone** transported from 10km (6mi) away. The scale of Nuraghic constructions varied greatly, depending on the function and importance of the buildings. Here, the fortress had a bastion with four towers at the corners.

Looking down inside the main tower

The bastion towers led to the courtyard through long corridors. The lower chamber at the end of a corridor is of the "tholos" type, where a "false cupola" was built by laying successive stones so that each course overhangs the previous one. To get here you have to negotiate narrow, dimly lit passageways and steps hewn from the rock.

From the top there are **superb views** of the whole site and of the more than 200 horseshoe-shaped roofless buildings of the surrounding Nuraghic village, some of which have now been reconstructed.

TAKING A BREAK

Have a coffee or a snack in the **bar** opposite the entrance to Su Nuraxi.

Parco Sardegna in Miniatura	✚ 176 A5 ✉ Su Nuraxi, Barúmini ☎ 070 920 9138
	🕐 Daily 9–dusk. Entry by guided tour only, running on the half hour
	👋 €10 (incl. Casa Zapata)

INSIDER INFO

■ Looming up behind Su Nuraxi is 🏠 **Giara di Gesturi**, a table mountain which is home to wild horses. A walk through the romantic countryside (cars are forbidden!) is unforgettable. Access roads at Gesturi and Tuili. Rangers offer horse rides and tours through the area (Centro Servizi Jara, Via G. B. Tuveri 16, Tuili; tel: 0709 364 277; www.parcodellagiara.it).

Insider Tip

■ Located at the foot of the volcanic cone Las Plassas is 🏠 **Parco Sardegna in Miniatura**. You can spend an unforgettable day in the park. Besides an extensive compound with its miniature copy of the island, which you can actually tour round on a boat, there are lots of further attractions. On the road from Tuili to Las Plassas (tel. 0709 36 10 04; www.sardegnainminiatura.it; April–Oct daily 9:30–7; miniature park only: €10, all attractions: €15).

Insider Tip

⭐6 Villasimíus

Lying in the far southeastern corner of the island, framed by *macchia* and pines, the former fishing village of Villasimíus is now a popular resort almost unfairly endowed with beautiful beaches nearby.

The main street in Villasimíus, Via Umberto I, widens out at the two main squares, Piazza Gramsci and Piazza Incani, at the heart of town. The **Ufficio Turistico** is located at Piazza Gramsci (tel: 070 793 0271; www.villasimiusweb.com) – a good place to pick up information on boat trips to the islands of Cávoli and Serpentara. Off Via Umberto I on Via Frau, the **Museo Archeológico** showcases local finds from Phoenician and Roman settlements and objects recovered from a 16th-century sunken ship.

Spiaggia Simius is the nearest beach, 1.5km (1mi) down Via del Mare. The high coast road north to **Costa Rei** is extraordinarily scenic, with glorious beaches along it, lapped by azure-green shallow seas. From here there are magnificent views of the offshore islands of **Cávoli and Serpentara**. Towards the south, the beach joins the Spiaggia Porto Giunco-Notteri, separating the sea from the lagoon of Notteri, which is frequently home to pink flamingos. On the western side the sands of Spiaggia del Riso are reminiscent of grains of white rice, hence the name "Riso" (rice). In fact they're minuscule pieces of translucent quartz.

The headland of **Capo Carbonara**, complete with old fortress and harbour, is the most southeasterly point of Sardinia. All the family will enjoy the 🛶 **boat trips** in this area.

▌TAKING A BREAK
The **Café del Porto** (➤ 64) by the marina is a good choice.

➕ 177 D1

Museo Archeológico
✉ Via Frau ☎ 070 793 0290
🕐 Tue–Thu 9–1, 4–6, Fri–Sun 10–1, 3–6, until 8 in high season 🎟 Free

There are beautiful beaches at Villasimíus

ⓘ Sárrabus

Only a few miles north of Villasimíus, the deserted Sárrabus mountains rise abruptly into a wild region of dense forests and *macchia*.

The rock formations of Monte dei Sette Fratelli

The rugged peaks of the **Monte dei Sette Fratelli** (Seven Brothers) rise to 1,023m (3,356ft). They are inhabited by some of the island's last remaining deer, the *cervo sardo*, who take cover under the mantle of fragrant *macchia*, cork and holm oak. Watch out for them when out 🚶 walking!

The winding and very scenic SS125 east of Cagliari goes north to the Monte dei Sette Fratelli. About 29km (18mi) out of Cagliari you come to a left fork for **Burcei**, famous for its cherry blossom in May. Opposite this turn-off is the Caserma Forestale. Here you can obtain maps of all the walks in the area, ranging from short mile-long loops to all-day treks.

Drive along the good 5km (3mi) long, unpaved forest road to the Giardino botánico Maidopis (free admission), Sardinian deer live here in enclosures. At **Castiádas**, there is a very good access point for the Monte dei Sette Fratelli, and the Cooperativa Monte dei Sette Fratelli here has a huge array of excursions on offer. The town was a penal colony in the 19th century, and the buildings have now been restored.

Insider Tip

The Sárrabus meets the sea at the little-known **Costa Rei**, a long string of glorious golden sand beaches between Punta di Santa Giusta and Capo Ferrato, and the less well-known, breathtaking Cala Sinzias.

TAKING A BREAK

Seek the shade of parasols on the terrace of **Marina Gio** (►64) enjoying a bounteous lunch overlooking the beach at Marina di San Giovani – with a beach bar in summer.

✚ 176 C/D2

⑫ Nora

In a setting surrounded by water, Nora is a time capsule of the island's early invaders. Phoenicians, Carthaginians and Romans all traded and lived here, and remains of two of those cultures are visible today.

Nora was the first settlement on the island to be founded by the Phoenicians in the eighth century BC. Strategically positioned on the Capo di Pula promontory, it had three harbours, so ensuring that at least one of them would be sheltered from the winds.

It was expanded by the Romans to become the most important city in Sardinia, but began to decline in the fifth century AD as increasing Arab raids forced inhabitants to the more easily defended hills of Cagliari. It was previously thought that the town was abandoned because of rising sea levels, but although a small part of the city now lies underwater, recent studies have proven that to be an unlikely reason for abandoning the site.

Ruins of the Roman amphitheatre

It is an evocative place, encircled by fragrant umbrella pines and overlooking a pretty beach. Most of the remains date to the Roman period. Highlights include the **theatre**, the only one on the island that staged plays rather than gladiatorial shows (it is still used for open-air concerts in summer), and the **Thermae** (baths) of which there were four.

Traces of Nora's Phoenician past are still visible. The earliest evidence found here are the steps from a **Nuraghic well**.

A long beach connects the historic site to the Byzantine-style church of **Sant'Efisio**, built in 1089 on the site where the saint was beheaded by Romans in AD303. The church is the destination of processions from Cagliari on 1 May (➤ 44, 66).

TAKING A BREAK

There's a restaurant and bar nearby, at **Sant'Efisio church**.

➕ 175 F1 ✉ Zona Archeológica
🕐 Daily 10–dusk 🎟 €7.50

At Your Leisure

⓭ Orto Botánico

Under a shady ficus tree, opposite a lily pond and fountain, the bronze bust of the founder, Patrizio Gennari (1820–97), greets you. This famous botanical garden has more than 500 species of tropical and Mediterranean plants. Among the exotic plants and trees bearing lemons the size of melons are the remains of Roman cisterns and an interesting display of medicinal or "curative" plants. It is a cool Cagliari retreat for a stroll among some prized specimens.

Insider Tip

✚ 176 B2 ✉ Viale Sant' Ignazio da Láconi
🛈 www.ccb-sardegna.it
🕐 Oct–March 9–11; April–Sep Mon–Fri 9–1, 3:30–7:30 💶 €2

⓮ Villanova

Villanova, on the eastern side of Cagliari, is modern and bustling and has a vibrant business quarter around Via S Giovanni. A great shopping route through this district is from Piazza Costituzione along Via Garibaldi, continuing on Via Paoli across Piazza San Benedetto and Via Dante Aligheri to Parco della Musica.

Insider Tip

The church of **San Domenico** was built in 1254. Severely bombed in 1943, it was largely rebuilt in 1954. However, there are still interesting parts of the old structure. These remains include the Chapel of the Rosario (1580) and the elaborate *chiostro* (cloister), three sides of which are fortunately intact, including the crypt, which contains parts of the late-Gothic building.

The **Basilica di San Saturnino** on Piazza San Cosimo is one of Sardinia's oldest churches. An example of Palaeo-Christian architecture, it was built in the fifth century in dedication to the Christian martyr Saturninus, who was killed on this spot during Emperor

Window balconies in Villanova

Diocletian's reign in AD304. It was later converted as a basilica in 1089. Recent excavation has revealed that it was originally a pre-Christian and then a Christian necropolis. The interior is stark and devoid of any decoration, but you can see the necropolis through the glass walls on either side of the nave.

✚ 176 B2

San Domenico
✉ Piazza San Domenico ☎ 070 662 837
🕐 By appointment only 8.15–11, 6–8.30

Basilica di San Saturnino
✉ Piazza San Cosimo (on the corner of Via Dante) ☎ 070 659 869
🕐 Tue–Sat 9–1 💶 Free

⓯ Castello di San Michele

The Spanish fortress stands atop a hill on the northwestern outskirts of Cagliari, in the middle of a large park. It started as a Byzantine tower in the 10th century and was expanded to include a Romanesque church (11th century), Pisan walls

(13th century) and, under the Catalans, two more towers (14th century). Its chequered history has included a spell as a luxurious residence belonging to the 15th-century Carroz family, who "acquired" decorative stone and marble pieces from the Basilica di San Saturnino to repair the castle's walls. During the great plague of 1652 it was a hospital. Today the complex is used for hosting events. The view from the Castello hill extends over the entire town to Poettostrand and the lagoon of Santa Gilla.

🕂 176 A2 ✉ Via Sirai
☎ 070 500 656; www.camuweb.it
🕐 June–Sep Tue–Sun 5–10; Oct–May daily 10–1, 3–6 🚌 City bus 5 💶 €3

16 🍴 Poetto & Marina Piccola

For sun, sand and relaxation, Poetto beach is the magnet for the local Cagliaritani and visitors alike. The almost 10km (6.2mi) stretch of soft, white sand lapped by clear, turquoise sea is beautifully framed by the mountains of the Sárrabus and Capo Carbonara. It is also backed by the lagoon of Molentargius, frequented by flamingos and many other species of wetland bird. At the southern end a rocky promontory, known as the Sella del Diávolo

Brightly painted beach huts at Poetto

(Devil's Saddle), rears above the marina. Legend has it that the Archangel Gabriel won a tussle with the Devil here and threw him off his *sella*, chasing him away with his band of angels – also giving the name Golfo degli Ángeli (Angels' Bay) to the Gulf of Cagliari. Loungers and parasols are available for rent and there are plenty of water sports available such as windsurfing, pedalos and canoes. The beach bristles with bars and cafés.

At the westernmost point of Poetto, Marina Piccola is also the liveliest part of the beach. Protected by the Sella del Diávolo promontory, the picturesque yacht basin is a fashionable local meeting place and sailing centre. In high summer there's a concert area and an open-air cinema.

🕂 176 B1
🚌 Buses PF, PQ from Piazza Matteotti

17 Ísola dei Cávoli

South of Villasimíus, the Capo Carbonara Protected Marine Area is a sea reserve protecting the coastline from Capo Boi to Punta de is Cappuccinus, including the idyllic little islands of Cávoli and Serpentara. However, it's still possible to take a boat trip to these islands as part of an excursion. The Ísola dei Cávoli is rather unpoetically

The nature reserve of the Costa Verde entices visitors with its secluded beaches

named "cabbage island", belying its castaway feel. A type of wild *cávoli* (cabbage) plant grows here in profusion together with Mediterranean *macchia*. From the granite rocks there are magnificent views across to swathes of white beaches as far as the Gulf of Cagliari. The rough, jagged coastline of granite rock is interspersed with tiny beaches, and the sea teems with marine life as it is now a protected marine park. Submerged in the water off the coast of the Ísola dei Cávoli lies a statue of the Madonna of shipwrecked sailors, to whom a feast day is dedicated, the *Festa della Madonna del Naufrago*. Every second Sunday of July a procession of boats reaches the location and a scuba priest recites a prayer at a depth of 10m (33ft).

🚩 177 D1 ☎ Boat trips on the historic schooner *Matilda* 340 067 6054/330 638 234; www.matildacharter.com ⏰ From the marina/port May–Sep daily (weather permitting) 10:30–4:30, with two stops for swimming 🎫 €50, lunch and drinks included

18 Ísola Serpentara

The island takes its name from its elongated shape as it snakes out along the sea, or possibly from the rare fly-trapping plant that flourishes on the island, the snake flower or *Helicodiceros muscivorus*. Like Cávoli, the island is granite rock covered with *macchia* and there is also a Spanish tower.

Cávoli island has been classified a Zone B protected area, which means scuba diving, fishing and unauthorized navigation are normally forbidden. Swimming and navigation with small, low-speed craft are permitted but fishing and scuba diving need official permission. The area of sea between Serpentara and Sardinia has been declared a Zone A Marine Park, which means it is totally protected and private boats are not allowed there.

🚩 177 D1 ℹ Permits: Area marina protetta Capo Carbonara, Via Roma 60, Villasimíus ☎ 070 790 234; www.ampcapocarbonara.it

19 Costa Verde

The pristine Costa Verde (Green Coast) in the southwest of the island is one of Italy's most important conservation areas and one of the most remote beach paradises on Sardinia. It is called "Sardinia's Sahara" because of its magnificent sand dunes. The only building is located at the mouth of the Riu Piscina in the middle of the "desert". It was the former loading point of a mining company, now the Hotel Le Dune. The access road passes through the deserted mining settlement Ingurtosu, a ghostly setting of decaying mining works and stockpiles.

Insider Tip   Just north of Buggerru is one of the island's not-to-be-missed golden beaches – **Spiaggia San Nicolò**, which is never crowded.
🔲 174 B5

Museo del Coltello Sardo
✉ Via Roma 15, Árbus
☎ 070 975 9220; www.museodelcoltello.it
🕐 Mon–Fri 9–12:30, 3:30–7; Sat, Sun by appointment 🎟 Free

20 Ísola di San Pietro
The very pretty Ísola di San Pietro is reached by a half-hour ferry ride from Portovesme. As the first sight of Carloforte comes into view, you could easily imagine yourself to be in mainland Italy's Liguria. Pastel-coloured houses cluster around the harbour, and the main street bears the name Via Genova. None of this is surprising when you discover that a colony of Genoese coral fishermen came here to settle in 1738; a version of old Genoese is still spoken today. Carloforte is famous throughout Italy for its tuna, which is served in many restaurants. Highlights of the area are the steep coasts of volcanic

trachyte encircling the spectacular Capo Sandolo as well as the impressive pointed cliffs on the Punta delle Colonne.
🔲 174 A2 🚢 Ferries from Portovesme: daily 5am–10pm; July, Aug until midnight; www.saremar.it
🎫 Foot passenger €2.50–€3, car €10–€12

21 Ísola di Sant' Antíoco
The island connected to the mainland by an embankment is a microcosm of nearly everyone who has controlled Sardinia, with Neolithic, Byzantine, Phoenician and Roman sites and artefacts to prove it. Locate the prehistoric sites on the interactive map at the excellent Antiquarium museum, whose collections include all the finds from the adjoining *tophet* where eighth-century BC Phoenicians and later Carthaginians buried the cremated remains of children.

From the little ethnographic museum, guides will take you to explore the astonishing Punic-era tombs carved into bedrock underneath the Savoy castle, some recycled as homes. More Phoenician-Punic connected tombs later became catacombs, and can be seen under the Basilica di Sant' Antíoco Martire below the castle.
🔲 174 B2

Leisure hours on the Piazza Repubblica in Carloforte on the Ísola di San Pietro

Torre di Chia guards Báia Chia (Costa del Sud)

Parco Archeológico

✉ Archeotur, Via Ugo Foscolo 4, Sant' Antíoco
☎ 0781 800 596; www.archeotur.it
🕐 Museo Archeológico and *tophet*: daily 9–7.
Museo Etnografico, Villaggio Ipogeo & Forte
Sabaudo: daily April–Sep 9–8; 1–15 Oct 9–1,
3:30–8; 16 Oct–March 9:30–1, 3–6
💶 €13 combined ticket (Museo Archeológico,
Tophet, Museo Etnografico, Villaggio Ipogeo &
Forte Sabaudo); €4–6 for individual sights.

🌄 Costa del Sud

Insider Tip Southwest of Cagliari, the coastal
road along the Costa del Sud is one
of the island's most scenic. It ser-
pentines upwards in numerous
curves and presents breathtaking
views of the cliffs and the sparkling
blue sea below. Then it descends
to the beaches, which are nestled
in the valleys cut into the cliffs. The
heart and hotspots of the Costa del
Sud are the fantastic beaches at
Báia Chia, with soft white sand and
dunes, partly flanked by lagoons
rich in local flora and fauna and
backed by juniper trees. You can
enjoy a superb view of the shimmering beach paradise fromTorre
di Chia, a 16th-century stone tower
that was once part of an imposing
network of sea defences to repel
Saracen pirates and invaders. You
can also admire the beauty and
variety of the coast in its entirety
if you walk out onto the Capo
Spartivento a promontory reaching
far out into the sea and home to a

The Basilica di Sant'Antíoco Martire on
the Ísola di Sant' Antíoco

former lighthouse (now probably
Sardinia's most unusual hotel).

Between Chia and Pula, the
Spiaggia di Santa Margherita
has a long white stretch of sand.
Concealed among the pine trees
are numerous hotels and resorts.
From Teulada it is only a few kilometres to 🌄 **Grotta Is Zuddas**, an
interesting dripstone cave. *Insider Tip*
➕ 175 D1

Ufficio Turistico

✉ Via Cagliari, Teulada
☎ 070 927 1230; www.comune.teulada.ca.it

Grotta Is Zuddas

✉ Loc. Is Zuddas, on the road to Santadi
☎ 0781 955 741; www.grotteiszuddas.com
🕐 Tours daily April–June 11, 12:15, 3, 4:15,
5:30; July–Sep 10–12:15, 2:30–6;
March, Oct noon–4 💶 €10

Where to...
Stay

Prices
Expect to pay for a double room per night:
€ under €90   €€ €90–€155   €€€ €155–€250   €€€€ over €250

CAGLIARI

Hotel A & R Bundes Jack Vittoria €–€€

In the heart of town, on the Via Roma with sea views, this historic building houses a two-star hotel on the third floor (with a lift). Established in 1938, the high ceilings, Murano glass, antique tiles, balconies, air-conditioned and spotless rooms and bathrooms give this family-run establishment more than a feel of faded elegance. For the best views, choose the sea-facing rooms with balconies, which carry a supplement. The family also runs the Bed and Breakfast Vittoria next door.

➕ 178 C3
✉ Via Roma 75
☎ 070 657 970; www.hotelbjvittoria.it

Miramare Boutique Hotel €€–€€€

Here you will find the very best in charm, romanticism and style. The 18 very tastefully and individually furnished rooms and four suites are on the first and second floor of the wonderful 18th-century Palazzo Devoto, which is located on the central Via Roma. It is one of the town's most impressive palazzi. Each room is dedicated to a *Giudice*, the princes from the golden period of Sardinia's independence and furnished accordingly. A small orchid house in the hotel displays orchids endemic to Sardinia. The diverse choice of dishes for breakfast is accompanied by a beautiful view of the harbour.

Insider Tip

➕ 178 B3 B Via Roma 59
☎ 070 664 021; www.hotelmiramarecagliari.it
🕐 All year

T Hotel €€€–€€€€

This is Cagliari's first designer hotel. The 15-floor steel and glass round tower opened in October 2005 after the famous Milanese architect Marco Piva had woven his magic, inspired by the colours of the south. There are 207 very stylish rooms themed on four different colours – vibrant orange, fiery red, relaxing green and tranquil blue – and all have spacious, airy bathrooms, glistening mosaic tiles and huge mirrors. The T Bistrot, combining style and good food, has become a popular meeting point, especially for Sunday brunch. The beauty and wellness centre is complete with an indoor pool. The hotel is on Piazza Giovanni XXIII in the heart of Cagliari, by the new Parco della Musica near the Teatro Lirico.

➕ 178 off C1   ✉ Via dei Giudicati 66
☎ 070 47400; www.thotel.it

VILLASIMÍUS

Hotel Mariposas €€–€€€€

The Mariposas is a small, very charmingly arranged hotel complex in neo-Sardinian style with 24 rooms and two junior suites in a fantastic location between Villasimíus and the beach. All of the rooms have a balcony or a terrace. There is a small pool in the well-kept garden. The sense of well-being that pervades the hotel has a lot to do with the cordiality and readiness to help of the owners – father and son.

✚ 177 D1
✉ Via Mar Nero 1
☎ 070 790 084; www.hotelmariposas.it

Stella Maris Hotel €€€

Overlooking Capo Carbonara on the southeastern tip of Sardinia, this hotel has a lovely setting, cradled in the bay of Campulongu. Attractive gardens lead down to the white sandy beach and there's also a freshwater swimming pool. Rooms are traditionally furnished and the best have sea views (supplement). The hotel is 3km (1.5mi) from the centre of Villasimíus.

✚ 177 D1
✉ Località Campulongu, Via dei Cedri 3
☎ 070 797 100; www.stella-maris.com

BARÚMINI

Hotel Su Nuraxi €

A stone's throw from Su Nuraxi, this hotel is simply furnished but has lovely views of the Giara plateau as well as the nuraghe. It is a good spot for lolling around in the *lolla* – a large Sardinian porch – taking in the views across waves of golden wheat fields. The restaurant serves traditional fare from land and sea, including *lumache alla diavola* (devilled snails), *troffiette speck funghi e noci* (pasta with raw ham, mushrooms and nuts) and entrecôte of beef or horse.

✚ 176 A5 ✉ On the street from Barúmini to Tuili approx. 1,000m to Su Nuraxi
☎ 070 936 8305; www.hotelsunuraxi.it

ÍSOLA DI SAN PIETRO

Hotel Riviera €€€

This terracotta-coloured building is a landmark on the harbour front and is the island's chicest hotel. It oozes style and comfort. All 44 rooms are very spacious

and individually decorated, complete with luxurious marble bathrooms. There is also an attractive rooftop terrace over-looking the harbour.

✚ 174 B2
✉ Corso Battellieri 26, Carloforte
☎ 0781 854 101;
www.hotelriviera-carloforte.com

ÍSOLA DI SANT' ANTÍOCO

B&B Gaulos Sant' Antíoco €

A small B&B close to the island's main sights – the Phoenician *tophet*, museum, castle, necropolis and catacombs. Guests can tour these on the bicycles provided by the B&B. Rooms are freshly renovated and comfortable, with en-suite facilities. The hosts have lots of suggestions for hidden beaches and little-known island secrets, such as a sea arch and nuraghi to explore.

✚ 174 B2 ✉ Via Goceano 45, Sant' Antioco
☎ 347 049 2487; www.gaulosbb.com

CHIA (DOMUS DE MARIA)

Hotel Spartivento €€–€€€

Embedded in a Mediterranean garden on the slopes overlooking the nearby beaches of Chia, this picturesque complex is an oasis of tranquillity and relaxation. 27 spacious, very beautifully furnished rooms, all with terrace and direct access to the garden. It is well worth booking a room with a view of the sea. The enchanting pool landscape offers total relaxation. On the covered panorama terrace of the hotel restaurant, waiters serve Italian and Sardinian delicacies. It is just a ten-minute walk to the beach. Tennis courts, a MTB rental service as well as a nearby 18-hole golf courts offer ample opportunities for sporting activities.

Insider Tip

✚ 175 E1 ✉ Località Chia,
Via Belvedere, Domus de Maria
☎ 070 92310; www.hotelspartivento.it
◯ Jan–Oct

Where to...
Eat and Drink

Prices
Expect to pay per person for a meal, excluding drinks:
€ under €26   €€ €26–€55   €€€ over €55

CAGLIARI

Dal Corsaro €€–€€€
This is a temple to gastronomy in elegant surroundings. The family-owned restaurant is an institution of the Cagliari culinary scene and attracts gourmets. Service is exemplary and the wine list is long.
✚ 178 D3 ✉ Viale Regina Margherita 28
☎ 070 664 318; www.dalcorsaro.com
🕓 Closed Jan

Dr Ampex €
This restaurant that is also popular with the locals has no menu; a fixed price of €25 brings course after course of delectable starters, a choice of main dish based on the freshest and best market ingredients, plus dessert, wine and *mirto*. A real delicacy, for instance, is the carpaccio of *bue rossa* (red ox) with slivered artichokes and mushrooms, or pasta with sea urchins, redolent of the Med. You won't find better value on the island.
✚ 178 D2 ✉ Via San Giacomo 35, Villanova
☎ 070 658 199
🕓 Tue–Sun 8pm–11pm, by reservation

Trattoria Da Serafino €–€€
Long-established, no-fuss trattoria: here you can try out traditional Sardinian cuisine at favourable prices, for example the *zuppa di cozze con arselle* or the Sardinian national dish *porceddu*, crispy suckling pig. At Serafino you will find a trattoria atmosphere. Very popular, and thus fairly loud.
✚ 178 C3 ✉ Via Lepanto 6 ☎ 070 651 795; www.trattoriadaserafino.com 🕓 Closed Thu

VILLASIMÍUS

Café del Porto €
In the modern café by the marina, you can savour delicious dishes while admiring the boats and also use the WLAN service. Happy hour is from 6:30 to 8:30pm in the restaurant/bar and piano bar, and the new disco bar buzzes from 10:30pm during the season.
✚ 177 D1 ✉ Porto di Villasimíus
☎ 070 797 8036 🕓 Daily 7am–2am

Marina Giò €–€€
About 2km (1.2mi) north of Muravera, this local favourite serves dishes that stretch the usual Sardinian repertoire a bit. Pizzas are prepared in a wood-fired oven, and ingredients for all dishes are sourced locally, in keeping with the island's traditions (►26). It's right on the beach, with ocean views and a terrace in the summer, when reservations are a good idea. *Insider Tip*
✚ 177 D1
✉ Marina di San Giovanni, Muravera
☎ 333 986 0200; www.marinagio.it
🕓 Tue–Sun 12:30–3, 7–midnight

Le Pavoncelle €€
Very inviting restaurant with a lovely atmosphere.
✚ 177 D1 ✉ Via Parigi 109 ☎ 070 791 273; www.lepavoncellevillasimius.it

Ristorante Carbonara €€
This traditional restaurant makes up for its rather lacklustre interior with large portions and very good fish. Recommendations include the homemade ravioli and the *spaghetti*

ai ricci di mare, spaghetti with sea urchin.

⊞ 177 D1 ⊠ Via Umberto I 60 ☎ 070 791 270; www.ristorantecarbonaravillasimius.com
Ⓒ Closed Tue

Stella Maris Hotel €€

There are two sea-facing restaurants at this hotel (►63), one inside and the other, al fresco with a veranda, has an especially beautiful location, with the sound of the water lapping and the rustling of the pine trees in the background. Fish is a speciality here, and there is a good wine list.

⊞ 177 D1 ⊠ Località Campulongu
☎ 070 797 100; www.stella-maris.com
Ⓒ 15 April to 30 Oct daily lunch and dinner

BARÚMINI

Sa Lolla Albergo Ristorante €€

This restaurant with rooms is in a country house with magnificent views over the Giara landscape. The pleasant rustic atmosphere is complemented by good food, specializing in seasonal Marmilla dishes.

⊞ 176 A5 ⊠ Via Cavour 49
☎ 070 936 8419; www.barumini.net/sa-lolla
Ⓒ Thu–Tue lunch and dinner

ÍSOLA DI SAN PIETRO

Da Nicolò €€€

An institution! A first-class restaurant managed by the well-known Luigi Pomata. Enjoy his *cucina carlofortina*, imaginative creations incorporating elements from Ligurian and North African cuisine, and with a focus on fish.

⊞ 174 B2 ⊠ In summer on the harbour promenade of Carloforte (Corso Cavour 32), in the pre-/post season in (Via Dante 32)
☎ 0781 854 048; www.danicolo.net
Ⓒ May–Sep, closed Mon

ÍSOLA DI SANT' ANTÍOCO

Ristorante Renzo e Rita €–€€

Sardinian specialities join a wider Mediterranean mix on the menu of this restaurant owned by the same family for generations. Expect only Sardinian wines, a list in which they take justifiable pride. The separate pizzeria prepares more than 40 different pizza toppings.

⊞ 174 B2
⊠ Via Nazionale 42, Sant' Antíoco
☎ 0781 800 448; www.renzoerita.com
Ⓒ 6pm–midnight, closed Wed

BUGGERRU

Pizzeria San Nicolò €–€€

This is a restaurant with a view if ever there was one. You look over the beach and the Capo Pecora. The restaurant specializes in the freshest grilled seafood, but the pastas and meat dishes are worth considering, too.

Insider Tip

⊞ 174 B4 ⊠ Località San Nicolò
☎ 0781 54359 Ⓒ Daily lunch and dinner

POETTO

Ristorante Dal Corsaro al Mare €€€

The first floor terrace restaurant has glorious views of the Golfo degli Ángeli. The speciality is seafood and, like its sister restaurant, Dal Corsaro (►64), it is a highly prized venue on the dining circuit. Downstairs there is the much less pricey but very good pizzeria **Spinnaker**.

⊞ 176 B1 ⊠ Località Marina Piccola
☎ 070 370 295; www.dalcorsaroalmare.it
Ⓒ May–Sep Tue–Sun lunch and dinner

PULA

Su Furriadroxu €

The inviting restaurant is in a cosy courtyard of an old Campidano farmhouse near the Piazza. Here you will find authentic Campidano cuisine. An additional highlight is the "Sa Piketada", an evening of Sardinian music and song.

⊞ 175 F2 ⊠ Via XXIV Maggio 11
☎ 070 924 6148; www.sufurriadroxu.it
Ⓒ Jan–Nov Thu–Mon 8pm–10:30pm

Where to...
Shop

BROWSING

Regardless of what you are looking for, on a shopping tour through Cagliari, you will find everything in abundance. Before you set off, it is worth cashing the necessary funds at a bank in Carlo Largo Felice. The tour begins at **Piazza Yenne** and continues through the pedestrian zone **Via Manno** and right across the Old Town. Then it's off along the **Via Garibaldi** and through the Villanova quarter. On the other side of the **Piazza Garibaldi,** stroll down the **Via Pola**, across **Piazza San Benedetto** and along **Via Dante Alighieri** to **Parco della Musica**, where you can take a breather by the fountains. **Via Roma** has some designer shops and the department store **Rinascente** (Mon–Fri 9–8:30, Sat 9–9, Sun 10–9). Sardinian specialities are sold in the Marina district, for example at **Sapori di Sardegna** (Vico dei Mille 1; www.saporidisardegna.com). The businesses are open from Mon–Sat 9–1, 5–8.

CRAFTS & CURIOS

Real Sardinian craftwork is best bought from **ISOLA** in Via Bacaredda 176, (tel: 070 492 756). A visit to the **Mercatino**, the colourful flea market between the Viale Trieste and the Viale Trento (Sun 8–2), is a real experience. Other flea markets are at the Bastione San Remy (Sun), Piazza del Carmine (1st Sun of month) and the Piazza Carlo Alberto (2nd & 4th Sun of the month). A visit to the Markthalle des **Mercato San Benedetto** is also fun (Via Cocco Ortu 50, buses no 1, 3, 6, 7; Mon–Fri 7–2, Sat 7–1:30, 5–8).

Where to...
Go Out

THEATRE & MUSIC

The main theatres in Cagliari are the **Teatro Lirico** (Via Sant'Alenixedda; tel: 070 408 2230; www.teatrolirico dicagliari.it) for opera, ballet and classical music; the **Teatro Massimo** (De Magistris 12; infopoint & tickets: Viale Trento, 9; tel: 070 279 6629-20; www.teatrostabiledellasardegna. it), staging classical theatre; and the **Exma** complex (Via San Lucifero 71; tel: 070 666 399), putting on concerts and exhibitions. The **Anfiteatro Romano** (tickets from Teatro Lirico) hosts open-air music and concerts. In the east of the city the **Fiera Campionaria** (Viale Diaz 221) has open-air rock concerts. Free listings are available from the tourist office.

NIGHTLIFE

Trendy meeting places in the Old Town are **Libarium Nostrum** (www.caffelibarium.com), **Caffè degli Spiriti** (www.caffedeglispiriti.com) and **San Remy** (www.cafesanremy.it). Popular locations include the disco-pub **Movida** (Viale Trieste 86), the **Donegal** with live music and a disco (Via Caprera 7) as well as the cool bar **Orus Cafe** (Viale Trieste 31). Cagliari's gay scene meets in the **Rainbow Fico d'India** on Poetto beach, in the small **Caffè Dell'Elfo** (Salita Santa Chiara 4/6) and in the **Go Fish** disco (Via Giovanni Battista Venturi 12).

FESTIVALS

Sardinia's biggest religious festival is the four-day **Festa di Sant'Efisio** (►40) in early May. The statue of Cagliari's patron saint, Efisio, leads a procession to Nora (►16).

Oristano & the West

 **Little Treats**

Unwind in the Thermal Baths
The 43°C (109°F) water from the **Fordongíanus thermal baths warmly** promises total relaxation: take a deep breath and forget everything else for a while (➤ 80).

Bathe in Paradise
You will feel like you are in paradise by the roaring **Cascata Sos Molinos** waterfall and natural pool near Santu Lussúrgiu (➤ 79).

Spend Time with the Fishermen
You can eat a delicious and reasonably priced meal at **Il Pescatore**, a simple restaurant on the beach of Marina di Torre Grande (➤ 78).

Getting Your Bearings

The fertile lowland region of Oristano through which Cedrino River flows constitutes, with Arborea, Sardinia's agricultural hub. In the west, the barren plains present quite a different picture. Dense forests await you in the verdant Monte Ferru and in the small mountain villages around the extinct volcano you will find authentic Sardinian customs. Around Monte Arci, the forests offer some wonderful hiking opportunities. Imposing Nuraghic edifices and spectacular holy wells await you here as do impressive evidence of foreign conquerors. The lively little town of Oristano and the coast are still relatively free of tourist hordes.

Sardinia's "Wild West" offers ample opportunity to encounter real Sardinians, be it at the traditional festivities and spectacular horse races or when sampling one of the many culinary specialities. Sardinia's best olive oil comes from here as does the tasty *bue rosso*. The little fishing village of Cabras is known for its seafood and its delicacy *bottarga*, the "Sardinian caviar" from the roe of the mullet. Traditional craftsmanship lives on in the villages. Impressive remnants of culture, such as the magnificent Nuraghic holy well of Santa Cristina or the Nuraghe Losa, the Roman baths in Fordongíanus and the imposing Roman city of Tharros on the peninsula of Sinis are what make the west of the island so interesting. What is more, the beaches mainly used by the locals are also very appealing, one example being the exceptional "rice corn" beaches on Sinis.

Ísola di
Mal di Ventre

Santa Maria della Neve, Cuglieri

TOP 10

Don't Miss

At Your Leisure

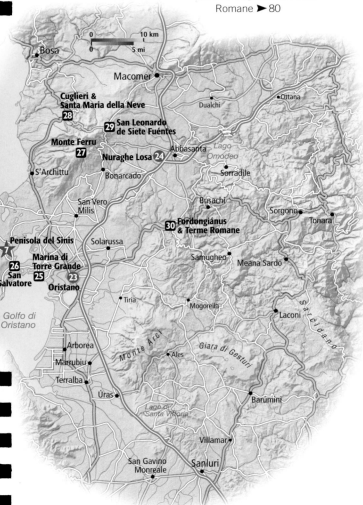

Perfect Days in...

Three Perfect Days

If you're not quite sure where to begin your travels, this itinerary recommends a practical and enjoyable three days exploring Oristano and the west of Sardinia, taking in some of the best places to see. For more information see the main entries (➤ 72–80).

Day 1

Morning
Buy delicacies as you wander through the centre of **23 Oristano** (photo above; ➤ 74) and visit the Antiquarium Arborense. Then go and have a swim near **25 Marina di Torre Grande** (➤ 78).

Lunch
Il Pescatore is perfect for lunch, a simple fish restaurant near the marina and directly by the beach.

Afternoon and Evening
After passing through the little fishing town of Cabras, which is surrounded by lagoons teeming with fish, the route continues via ⭐**Penisola del Sinis** (right; ➤ 72) to **26 San Salvatore** (➤ 78) and San Giovanni di Sinis. There you can admire the early Christian church of San Giovanni before passing through the ancient town of **Tharros** (➤ 73). After stopping off for a swim at the "Rice Corn" beach at Is Arutas and a refreshing drink at one of the two simple beach bars, you can return to Oristano, in order to try out the specialities of the regional cuisine at **Cocco e Dessi** and then spend the night at **Hotel Il Duomo** (➤ 81).

Day 2

Morning

From Oristano continue on SS131 to Abbasanta. On the way, don't forget to visit the Nuraghic holy well Santa Cristina and **24 Nuraghe Losa** (➤ 76)! From Abbasanta continue on the SP15 into the mountain village of Santu Lussúrgiu, where you can visit the cutlers in the Mura family.

Lunch

Try the gastronomic delights at **Sas Benas** (Piazza San Giovanni; tel: 0783 550 870, www.sasbenas.it) in the centre of Santu Lussúrgiu.

Afternoon

From Santu Lussúrgiu, you soon reach **29 San Leonardo de Siete Fuéntes** (➤ 80), where springs babble through the shade of the groves. Beautiful landscape accompanies the SP19 to **28 Cuglieri** (➤ 80), curving through the dense foret of **27 Monte Ferru** (➤ 79). You can eat well and find good accommodation in **Caponieddu** (Podere n. 1 zona ex Etfas di Santa Caterina di Pittinuri, 09073 Cuglieri, Oristano; tel: 0785 850 493, www.caponieddu.it).

Day 3

Morning

From Pittinuri follow the road to **28 Cuglieri** and Tresnuraghes to Suni, which is well-known for its basket weaving and then on the SS129 to Macomer, the centre of the island's cheese production. After visiting the *zona archeólogica Tamuli* (towards Santu Lussúrgiu), you drive along the SS131 to Ghilarza.

Afternoon

Along the west bank of the reservoir, the road takes you into the Valley of Tirso to **30 Fordongiánus** (➤ 80) and its Roman thermal baths. After a picnic and a dip in the hot springs, take the SS388 back to Oristano.

Cuglieri &
Santa Maria della Neve
28   **29** San Leonardo
de Siete Fuéntes
27   **24** Nuraghe Losa
Monte Ferru

Penisola del Sinis   **30** Fordongiánus
7 Marina di   & Terme Romane
San **26** Torre Grande
Salvatore **25** **23** Oristano

⭐ Penisola del Sinis

This low-lying peninsula west of Oristano is a watery wonderland full of large lagoons. Tharros appealed to the Phoenicians because its location made it a good place for a harbour, although they were probably also impressed by the beauty of the narrow peninsula jutting far out into the ocean. Testimony to its history is provided by a Spanish watchtower looming over the town.

The huge **Stagni**, shallow lagoons between the peninsula and Cabras are famous for their abundance of fish and different birds. Over 150 species of bird have been spotted here, including the colourful purple swamphen. In spring and autumn, the birdlife is particularly impressive when hundreds of migrating birds visit either to stay for the winter or to build up their strength for the next part of their journey. Throughout the year, you will see the *Sa Genti Arrubia* ("the red people"), as the Sardinians call the flamingos, on the island.

The other claim to fame of the otherwise rather unspectacular little fishing town of **Cabras** is its reputation as Sardinia's mecca for friends of the lagoon's seafood cuisine. It is also regarded as a centre for *bottarga*, Sardinia's caviar, as the lagoon is full of mullet whose roe is used for this speciality.

Insider Tip

The **Museo Archeológico** exhibits the magnificent "Giants of Cabras". The huge statues, which weigh up to 400kg (63 stone) were discovered in a tomb complex by Monte Prama in 1974 and stored for decades unnoticed in the cellar before work started on their restoration. They are now regarded as a sensational archaeological find. The 39 sandstone figures that have so far been put together from the broken pieces probably date back to the ninth or eighth century BC.

The extensive excavation site of the Roman harbour town at Tharros

Tharros

Lying 20km (12mi) west of Oristano, this is one of the island's **top archaeological sites**. It wasn't until 1956 that excavations began in earnest to reveal this prosperous Phoenician port dating back to 730BC. Although most of what is now visible belongs to the Roman period, there are still remnants of the Phoenician city in a temple with Doric half-columns and, north of the main site, a *tophet*, a site where burnt offerings were made and where archaeologists found many urns containing the remains of children.

The Roman city had the usual shops, taverns, baths and amphitheatre. At the northern end you will find a relatively modest second to third century AD example of this, partially occupying the area of the *tophet*. Gladiatorial and wild beast contests were staged here for the delight of up to 8,000 people during the Roman era. Nowadays, there are **open-air performances** on a makeshift stage by the sea in high season. Sunset at Tharros is a magical experience.

Tharros' **Torre di San Giovanni** (9am–sunset) can be climbed for spectacular views – depending on wind conditions. It is not without reason that Tharros is known as being on the windy peninsula.

🞢 170 C3 ☎ 0783 370 019; www.penisoladelsinis.it
🕐 Apr–Oct daily 9–8; Nov–March 9–5
💶 €5, €7 (incl. Museo Cívico in Cabras)

Museo Archeológico Cabras

The peninsula stretches far out into the sea

✉ Via Tharros 121 ☎ 0783 290 636
🕐 Apr–Oct daily 9–1, 4–8; Nov–March 9–1, 3–7
💶 €5

㉒ Oristano

The unpretentious, lively provincial capital, Oristano, used to be the centre of the judiciary of Arborea and the residence of the regent and Sardinia's national hero Eleonora von Arborea. It is here that the colourful Sa Sartiglia festival has taken place since 1546. Oristano was originally built using the stone from the nearby Roman harbour town of Tharros.

Evidence of human habitation in this area dates right back to the sixth millennium BC before the Nuraghic civilization began to spread. By the ninth century BC the first Phoenician merchants landed at Tharros, on the coast of Sinis. Tharros was later abandoned to escape the increasingly frequent raids by the Moors. As the local expression goes, "*Portant de Tharros sa perda a carros*" ("They're bringing cart-loads of stones from Tharros") – to build the new town, originally named Aristanis, meaning "between the ponds".

Oristano reached a new zenith during the Middle Ages under the regency of the legendary Eleonora di Arborea. In the ensuing struggle between Pisa and Aragon, the town sided with Aragon and centuries of economic neglect followed. However, the town is now reviving its fortunes and is Sardinia's fourth provincial capital and agricultural centre.

The heart and soul of the Old Town is the beautiful **Piazza Eleonora** that is surrounded by magnificent old palazzi. In the middle of the square stands a statue of the national hero Eleonora von Arborea.

Archaeological Museum

From the Piazza Eleonora it is just 150m to the **Antiquarium Arborense**. This is home to one of the island's top archaeological collections, with displays spanning prehistoric, Nuraghic, Phoenician and Roman treasures. On the ground floor a fourth-century BC **lion** from Tharros (►73) greets you. There are **tiny ivory dice**, a green jasper scarab dating from the sixth century BC and numerous figurines and **ceramics**. There are masks, too, recovered from Tharros, to keep the evil eye at bay – "apotropaic" masks put in beside the dead

The onion-domed tower of the Duomo stands out above the houses of Oristano

in Punic times to cast away evil spirits. Some of the grimacing faces are enough to scare the life out of you. There are also human bones (fifth to first century BC) and terracotta urns with the remains of stillborn babies from fourth-century Tharros. On the first floor you can see a **model of Roman Tharros** as it probably appeared in the fourth century AD.

Duomo

The Duomo (cathedral) is the largest in Sardinia and is devoted to Santa Maria Assunta. Although founded in the 12th century, its current style is the result of an 18th-century reconstruction. However, inside are the remaining Gothic vestiges of the groin-vaulted **Rimedio Chapel** in the right transept. Look out, too, for the 14th-century **Annunciation** by Nino Pisano and fragments of a **medieval marble pulpit** depicting Daniel in the Lions' Den. The onion-domed campanile is a symbol of the Oristano skyline.

TAKING A BREAK

Enjoy a glass or two of Oristano's famous Vernaccia dessert wine at the **Caffè Shardana** on Piazza Eleonora.

➕ 170 C2

Antiquarium Arborense
✉ Piazzetta Corrias
☎ 0783 791 262; www.antiquariumarborense.it
🕐 Mon–Fri 9–8, Sat, Sun 9–2 💶 €5

Duomo
✉ Piazza Duomo
🕐 Mon–Sat 8:30–7:30, Sun 10–noon and 6

INSIDER INFO

Vivid impressions of **Sa Sartiglia** (➤ 20) are available at the Centro Documentazione della Sartiglia (Piazza Eleonora; tel: 0783 303 159; www.sartiglia.info; summer: 10–1, 5–8:30; Mon–Sat 10:30–1, 5–7:30 rest of year).

Insider Tip

㉔ Nuraghe Losa

Just a couple of miles west of the Carlo Felice highway (SS131), this huge megalithic monument looms into view. It is one of Sardinia's most important and best-preserved monuments of the Nuraghic civilization.

Encircled by two large walls – the inner one with small towers – it is built of great basalt blocks and is estimated to be more than 3,500 years old. Easily accessible, this symbol of silence lies in splendid isolation on a grassy site, but within view of the main road.

Nuraghe Losa is a superb monument

The Construction

The **nuraghe** has a truncated cone or beehive shape, built in the distinctive Cyclopean style, which used no mortar – nor indeed any other binding material – but was erected entirely by piling up huge blocks. The central tower, 13m (43ft) high and 12.5m (41ft) wide, originally had three floors and, almost certainly, a corbelled top, long since destroyed.

A narrow stone corridor gives access to two of the original three floors of the topless central tower and several ancillary buildings dotted around the site. The tall conical interior is illuminated by sunken lighting and the walls are peppered with niches and alcoves. Around it there are other later towers, enclosed in an imposing triangular curtain and surrounded and fortified by defensive walls

INSIDER INFO

Ghilarza, close to Abbasanta, was the boyhood home of **Antonio Gramsci**, the celebrated Marxist writer, politician and philosopher (1891–1937). His small home in the centre is the **Casa Museo di Antonio Gramsci** (Corso Umberto 36; tel: 0785 54164; www. casagramscighilarza.org; Fri–Wed 10–1, 2–7; admission free).

with towers and arrow-slits estimated to date to around the seventh century BC. Winding stone steps lead up to a terrace from where there are splendid views over the high plain and, to the east, as far as Gennargentu on a good visibility day.

Successive Settlements

As always, the exact origins and functions of these monuments are shrouded in the mists of time. Today there is evidence of an **unexcavated prehistoric village** around the perimeter wall and, inside the main entrance to the site, cinerary urns from the first to second century AD. It is probable that in the post-Nuraghic phase the Phoenicians, Romans and possibly also Byzantines took it over as a fortress. What is known is that the whole "village" was continuously occupied from its middle Bronze Age origins to the seventh century AD. This peaceful, yet eerie, site is the perfect place to let your imagination roam.

An interior view of the nuraghe

There is a little museum here with a few artefacts, such as pottery and vases, which were found within the area, but the major finds are in Cagliari's Archaeological Museum (▶ 51). Also in the museum are maps showing the locations of other nuraghi and ancient sites.

TAKING A BREAK

A sight in its own right is the superb **Stone Art Café** in Ghilarza (Via del Mandrolisai 100; tel: 347 999 5735, www.stone-art.it; Mon–Sat 6:30am–9pm). It is the fanciful creation of two young stone masons from Abbasanta.

Insider Tip

🔳 171 E4

✉ Parco Archeológico Nuraghe Losa, directly next to the SS131 "Carlo Felice", between Km123 and Km124

☎ 329 726 0732; www.nuraghelosa.net

🕐 Daily 9 till dusk

✋ €5

At Your Leisure

25 🛈 Marina di Torre Grande

Named after the Aragonese watch-tower that stands sentinel over it, this is the most majestic of all towers erected by the Spanish, built at the end of the 16th century to protect the Sardinian coasts from pirates. The pine- and palm-fronted esplanade faces a wide beach of fine blonde sand, especially child-friendly as it shelves gradually into the sea.

The beach is also well known on the windsurfing circuit. If you prefer to watch others carving creamy wakes across the water, the esplanade is a good spot to linger in one of the many bars and cafés that line the shore. By night the resort really buzzes after the obligatory *passeggiata* along the Lungomare Eleonora d'Arborea. Out of season the whole resort is deserted with the melancholy air of a ghost town. A little farther south on the Golf of Oristano is the **Spiaggia di San Giovanni di Sinis**. More exposed, this is a good spot for surf, clean, deep sea and fine, white sand.

➕ 170 C2

26 San Salvatore

Off the Tharros road, 6km (4mi) west of Marina di Torre Grande is San Salvatore church, which is surrounded by *cumbessias*, small pilgrim dwellings. Beneath the church lies the **hypogeum**, a subterranean complex, which was used as a place of worship even during the Nuraghic era and then later for holding the church services of early Christian communities. The complex surrounded by a high wall is reminiscent of a small Mexican village from a "spaghetti western" film. Indeed, San Salvatore

A quiet street in San Salvatore, scene of the annual Corsa degli Scalzi

has served as the location for quite a few Italian Westerns!

Once a year for the **Corsa degli Scalzi (Barefoot Race)**, sleepy San Salvatore is shaken from its slumber. In the early morning hours of the first Saturday in September, a group of barefoot men take the statue of the saint and carry it for 6km (4mi) to the church of San Salvatore. On the following day, the barefoot men clad in white tunics run with the statue back to Cabras. This famous religious festival, which is accompanied by nine days of festivities, dates back to 1619 when the saint's statue was rushed to safety to protect it from the Saracens..

In the hamlet of **San Giovanni di Sinis** stands a small church of the same name. It is one of the oldest and probably most beautiful religious buildings in Sardinia. This early Christian building was built in the fifth century with a Byzantine cupola ceiling. A nave and transept were added in the ninth century.

Almost opposite is the Visitor Centre of the **Marine Protected Area**, an area which encompasses the majority of the Sinis coast and the adjacent bird island Ísola Mal di Ventre (www.areamarinasinis.it).
✚ 171 C2

27 Monte Ferru

Densely forested and verdant Monte Ferru (Iron Mountain) is an extinct volcano that rises 1,050m (3,445ft) to its peak **Monte Urtigu**. The surrounding villages are renowned for their handicrafts *Insider Tip* and their specialities. **Santu Lussúrgiu** boasts leather workshops, such as the Spanu saddlery (www.selleriaspanu.it), and traditional cutlers such as the Coltelleria Mura (Viale Azuni 29) that has been in the business for generations, as well as a distillery whose *Abbardente* is one of the best aquavits in Sardinia (www.abbardente.it). In the neigh-

A detail of the painted dome of the Chiesa di San Sebastiano in Seneghe

bouring **Seneghe**, which proudly calls itself "*Città di Olio*", you will find the best olive oil on the island. Azienda Agricola Cosseddu produces top quality at reasonable prices. You can buy the multi-award-winning oil directly from the family (Via Josto 13). Just a few paces away, well-known musician Raymond Usai makes, plays and sells Sardinian musical instruments of the most varied kind, for example the well-known shepherd's flute *launeddas*, an instrument that has been used since the Stone Age. (www.urm-sonosdesardigna.com).

Finally, in **Bonarcado** you will find one of the few butchers allowed to slaughter and sell the *bue rosso*, a huge red ox, an ancient native breed from Monte Ferru with exceptionally tender meat (www.macelleriasassu.it).

Near San Leonardo di Siete Fuéntes

28 Cuglieri & Santa Maria della Neve

Halfway up the slopes of Monte Ferru, this important agricultural town is, along with Seneghe, the leading producer of excellent olive oil. The silver dome of the 15th-century Santa Maria della Neve is visible from miles around. From the basilica's churchyard there are sublime views of the coast, as far as the cliffs of Porto Conte near Alghero on a clear day.
✚ 170 C4

29 San Leonardo de Siete Fuéntes

True to its name, there are seven springs in this shady grove and seven taps from which to imbibe the mineral waters. They have a diuretic effect and some are mildly radio-active, but supposedly have great healing powers. The Romanesque Chiesa di San Leonardo, hewn out of dark trachyte rock, was built in the 12th century by the Knights of St John of Jerusalem. They once ran a hospital next door, where Guelfo, son of Count Ugolino della Gherardesca, died in 1292. He is buried here.
✚ 170 D4

30 Fordongiánus & Terme Romane

South of Lake Omodeo is the spa town of Fordongiánus. The Romans set up their spa here, and it's still possible to visit the first century AD bath complex. The water that gushes up is a scalding 54ºC (129ºF), and clouds of steam rise from the river. The town is bathed in a russet glow from the local red trachyte stone, a good example of which is the 16th-century Casa Aragonese. On the opposite side of the river towers the modern façade of the **Grand-Hotels SPA Terme di Sardegna** (www.termesardegna.it). More fun and just as relaxing is a dip in the old 31 **Bagni Termali** opened in 1800 located just a few steps further up the river.

Insider Tip

✚ 171 E3

Bagni Termali
🕓 Summer daily 9:30–12:30, 3:30–7
🎫 €4; €5 on Sun

Terme Romane
☎ 0783 60157; www.forumtraiani.it
🕓 Summer daily 9–1, 3:30–7; winter 9:30–1, 2:30–5 🎫 €4

Casa Aragonese
🕓 Apr–Sep Tue–Sun 9:30–1, 3–7:30; Oct–March 9:30–1, 3–5:30 🎫 €4

Where to...
Stay

Prices
Expect to pay for a double room per night:
€ under €90 **€€** €90–€155 **€€€** €155–€250 **€€€€** over €250

ORISTANO

Hotel Domus De Logu €€€
Ten stylishly furnished junior suites and two mini apartments in a magnificent Art Nouveau Palazzo. Breakfast is served in your room.
➕ 170 C2 ✉ Piazza Mariano 50
☎ 0783 360 102, www.hddl.eu

Mistral €–€€
There are two hotels of this name in Oristano. This is the smaller and less expensive of the two. It is located in the historical centre in a quiet side street. Modern and well-equipped, the hotel has 48 rooms and a good restaurant that serves regional specialities.
➕ 170 C2 ✉ Via Martiri di Belfiore 2
☎ 0783 212505; www.hotelmistraloristano.it/en

PENISOLA DEL SINIS/RIOLA SARDO

Hotel da Cesare €–€€
The location is its highlight: Putzu Idu is a sleepy hamlet, Cesare an older establishment. The 18 rooms are simply furnished, but the hotel is just a stone's throw from the beach. Offering a spectacular terrace with wonderful sunsets, it is the ideal spot for those fleeing civilization for a while. *Insider Tip*
➕ 170 B3 ✉ Via Lungomare, Putzu Idu
☎ 0783 52095, www.hoteldacesare.com

Hotel Lucrezia €€–€€€
Behind the long wall lies a haven of peace, with wonderful tranquil gardens full of flowers, trees, wells and Vernaccia barrels. It is the old farmstead of the grandfather, which the grandson has transformed into a very charming little hotel. There are seven extremely stylishly furnished rooms and, in its own little house in the garden, one suite. It is simply wonderful here and you will not want to leave! *Insider Tip*
➕ 170 C3 ✉ Via Roma 14a, Riola Sardo
☎ 0783 412 078; www.hotellucrezia.it

Sa Pedrera €–€€
Lying about 8km (5mi) out of Cabras, en route to San Giovanni di Sinis, this stone *casa coloniale campidanese*, or typical Sardinian hacienda-style hotel, is an oasis of cool. Rooms are simply but comfortably furnished and surrounded by attractive gardens. Excellent beaches are nearby.
➕ 162 B3 ✉ SP Cabras–S Giovanni di Sinis Km 7.5 ☎ 0783 370 018; www.sapedrera.it

Hotel Villa Canu €€
23 pretty rooms, decorated in typical Sardinian style (18 of which have direct access to the secluded patio garden) in an old *casa campidanese* in the middle of the Old Town. The hotel has its own restaurant: Il Caminetto (► 83).
➕ 170 C3 ✉ Via Firenze 9, Capras
☎ 0783 290 155, www.hotelvillacanu.com

NURAGHE LOSA

Mandra Edera Farm €€
A country residence for equestrian fans, wonderfully tranquil and located in the middle of nowhere. The bungalows scattered over the extensive grounds offer in total four spacious, nicely appointed rooms

and eight suites. A pool for relaxation and lots of horses.

➕ 171 E4 ✉ Via Dante 20, Abbasanta
☎ 320 151 5170; www.mandraedera.cc

Sa Mola €€

Tranquil idyll offering excellent cuisine (► 83) and charming bungalows, nestled in a large park with a manor house and old oil mill. All of the rooms have a covered terrace facing out onto the garden.

➕ 171 D4 ✉ Via Giardini, Bonarcado
☎ 0783 56588; www.samola.it

SANTU LUSSÚRGIU

Antica Dimora del Gruccione €€

This lovely 17th-century mansion is Spanish in design and filled with antiques. Owner Gabriella Belloni named it after the *gruccione*, a bird that migrates in the summer to Sardinia from the tropics. Every time that Gabriella returned to Santu Lussúrgiu for the summer season to visit her grandparents' house, the *gruccione* was there. This is an *albergo diffuso*, consisting of a main mansion and several other buildings in the neighbourhood. All rooms are individually decorated.

➕ 171 D4 ✉ Via Michele Obinu 31
☎ 0783 552 035; www.anticadimora.com

CUGLIERI

Hotel La Baja €€–€€€

The hotel may not look very appealing from the outside, but its prominent position high up on the picturesque cliff tops is absolutely sensational. All of the 29 rooms have balconies with an enchanting view of the coast and sea.

➕ 170 C4
✉ Via Scirocco 20, Santa Caterina di Pittinuri
☎ 0785 389 149; www.hotellabaja.it

Hotel Desogos €

Set in the heart of Cuglieri's Old Town, this a convenient stopping-off point while exploring the area.

The small hotel is comfortable but plainly furnished and rooms are available with or without bathrooms en suite. The restaurant is very good indeed and attracts a lot of locals. This *ristorante/ albergo* ("restaurant with rooms") is family run and is very good value for money.

Insider Tip

➕ 170 C4
✉ Vico Cugia 6 (off the main Via Cugia one-way street through the Old Town)
☎ 0785 39660

FORDONGIÁNUS

Sardegna Grand Hotel Terme €€€

This modern spa hotel has comfortable air-conditioned rooms with balconies. There are many different treatments on offer for an extra cost, including Ayurvedic massage, mudpacks, reflexology and bathing in the mineral waters. The hotel lies on the other side of the river from the Terme Romane.

➕ 171 E3 ✉ Strada Provinciale 48, n.1
☎ 0783 605 016; www.termesardegna.it

LAKE OMODEO

Villa Asfodeli €–€€

This Art Nouveau villa nestled in a Mediterranean garden with a pool could be rightly called a "hotel de charme". Shared between three buildings, some of the 14 tastefully furnished rooms enjoy a wonderful view of the coast 5km (3mi) away. Suite no. 122 on the second floor with its very large panorama terrace is particularly outstanding. The bike-friendly establishment can provide rental bikes and all the accoutrements needed for a cycling holiday at www.sardinia biketour.it. Very friendly staff, good and hearty breakfast. Only slight hiccup: the hotel does not have a restaurant.

➕ 170 C4/5
✉ Piazza Giovanni XXIII n. 4, Tresnuraghes
☎ 0785 315 052; www.asfodelihotel.com

Where to...
Eat and Drink

Prices
Expect to pay per person for a meal, excluding drinks:
€ under €26   €€ €26–€55   €€€ over €55

ORISTANO

Cocco & Dessì €€
Innovative cuisine served in several dining spaces, including a gazebo, in this traditional 1925 restaurant. The menu includes seasonal specialities. Also pizzas in the evening.
⊞ 170 C2 ✉ Via Tirso 31 ☎ 0783 252 648; www.coccoedessi.it ⊕ Tue–Sun lunch lunch; closed Sun eve and three weeks in Jan

Osteria del Vicolo €
Family-run restaurant in the centre of the Old Town. Worth special mention is the buffet, which offers a good range of vegetarian dishes. The dining area is decorated with contemporary artworks.
⊞ 170 C2 ✉ Vico Episcopio 14
☎ 340 143 3700; www.osteriadelvicoloristano.it

Craf Da Banane €–€€
This popular restaurant offers traditional Sardinian food in a refined, yet relaxed setting. Fish dishes are naturally among the menu's highlights. Good choices include sea bass or pasta with mussels, both of which can be savoured with a glass or two of local white wine.
⊞ 170 C2 ✉ Via de Castro S.A. 34
☎ 0783 70669; www.ristorantecrafdabanana.com ⊕ Mon–Sat lunch and dinner; closed Sun

PENISOLA DEL SINIS

Il Caminetto €€
The menu here specializes in fish and seafood. Mullet features, not just *bottarga* (roe) but also *sa merca* (salted and cooked in herbs) or *affumicato* (smoked).

⊞ 170 C3 ✉ Via Cesare Battisti 8, Cabras
☎ 0783 391 139; www.hotelvillacanu.com
⊕ Tue–Sun lunch and dinner

Le Dune €€
Cosy and intimate restaurant with a good selection of seafood at reasonable prices. The owner is happy to give details of what has been freshly caught on the day.
⊞ 170 C2 ✉ Via Chiesa 1, San Giovanni di Sinis
☎ 0783 370 089; www.ristoranteledune.it
⊕ June–Sep daily lunch and dinner;
Oct–May lunch only

BONARCADO

Sa Mola €–€€
As you might expect from Sardinia's passion for locally produced foods, this excellent restaurant is part of the Slow Food movement. Find local *cinghiale* (wild boar) served as a carpaccio, and local beef prepared with wild mushrooms and Sardinian wine. The pizzas are also good.
⊞ 171 D4 ✉ Via Giardini ☎ 0783 56588;
www.samola.it ⊕ Mon–Sat lunch and dinner

MONTE FERRU/SENEGHE

Sa Tanka €€
In addition to many other seasonal specialities used in the wide choice of dishes for which the restaurant has made itself a name, the rare *bue rosso* is also served here. You can also buy delicious lunch packets for a picnic here.
⊞ 171 D3 ✉ Piazzale Montiferru 3–4, Seneghe
☎ 0783 54004; www.satanka.it
⊕ 13 June to 15 Sep Tue–Sun lunch and dinner;
Fri–Sun rest of year

Insider Tip

Insider Tip

Where to...
Shop

In **Oristano** there are morning markets in **Via Mazzini** and **Via Costa** (Mon–Sat) and on the first Saturday of the month there's an antiques and bric-a-brac market in **Piazza Eleonora**. The area is renowned for its white Vernaccia wine, and the **Cantina Sociale della Vernaccia** is at Via Oristano 6, Rimedio (tel: 0783 33383; www.vinovernaccia. com; Mon–Fri 8–1, 3:30–6). Local winegrowers bring their grapes here to be crushed. The main shopping promenade of the town is the pedestrian area Via Lamarmora. The market hall (Mon–Sat 7–1) in der Via Mazzini sells everything that the region produces. An **ISOLA** centre for ceramics is in the Via Cagliari, on the corner of Via del Porto.

Buy *bottarga* in **Cabras** near **Spanu** in the Via Carducci (www. spanubottarga.com), multi-award-winning olive oil in Seneghe from the **Cosseddu family** (Via Josto 13).

Santu Lussúrgiu is famous for its cutlers and upholsterers. Handmade knives are on sale at **Coltelleria Mura** (Via Azuni 1), handmade leather ware, especially riding accessories, in the **Selleria Spanu** (Via Dei Monti Lussurgesi 5, www.selleriaspanu.it). A very good grappa is available at the **Lussurgesi distillery** (Via die Sogenti 14, www. abbardente.it).

Bue rosso meat is on sale at the **Macelleria Sassu** in **Bonacardo** (Via Torino 1, www.macelleriasassu.it).

The cheese speciality *casizolu di monteferru* made from cow milk is available in **Cuglieri** from **Appiu** (Corso Umberto 2).

The citrus fruit oasis of **Milis** produces Sardinia's best oranges for 10 months of the year. There is a weekly market every Wednesday.

Where to...
Go Out

TOURS & EXCURSIONS

Tourist information and a wide selection of tours and excursions covering the entire Oristano region are available from the **Ufficio Turismo** (Piazza Eleonora 19; tel: 0783 36831, www.gooristano. com; Mon–Thu 8:30–1, 3–6, Fri 8:30–1).

NIGHTLIFE

For those who enjoy lively nightlife venues, **Oristano** is the best choice. It has a very good choice of fun bars that stay open late. Among the top spots is the stylish **Lola Mundo** café (Piazzetta Corrias 14), which is open until 1am Friday and Saturday and until 9 on other weekdays.

On Via Ghilarza there are clubs that are open in winter only, such as **Ovest** (Via Ghilarza 5), which is open on Friday and Saturday from 11pm.

One of Sardinia's biggest dance temples is **Le Saline** (Oasi Sale Porcus, SP10, Km 12.6; www. lesalinemeeting.com) on the road to Putzu Idu.

Another long-time favourite for night owls is the **Emotional Disco Club** on the SP6 near San Salvatore at Km 7 (www.sapedreradisco.it, every Fr).

Along the SP292 are three popular clubs: **La Capanna** in Torre del Pozzo as well as the **Menhir** and **Energie** – the latter two are in Santa Caterina di Pittinuri.

On the coast at **Marina di Torre Grande**, bars and clubs line the esplanade in summer, including the top locations **Coco Loco**, **Oasi**, **Moby Dick**, **Nelson** and **Maripa**.

Núoro & the East

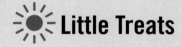 **Little Treats**

An Open-Air Museum as an Oasis
You can escape the heat of the sun at
the open-air museum **S'Abba Frisca** by
an old mill, where cool water is available
in abundance (➤ 96).

Siesta at Sardinia's Most Powerful Spring
The sparkling **Su Gologne** spring, embedded
in shady groves, is a great place for a picnic
and a siesta (➤ 96).

Eat with the Shepherds
A meal under the enormous oaks of **Pratobello**
is unforgettable – the shepherds of Orgosolo
invite you to dine with them (➤ 97).

Getting Your Bearings

In the heart of the island rise the highest mountains of the Gennargentu. Known today as the Barbagia, this part of Sardinia was never conquered by invaders. This is a land of shepherds, pastoral farming, dramatic scenery and tradition, where villages are few and far between. It also has a wildly beautiful coastline indented with idyllic coves, grottoes and caves, and glorious beaches of pristine white sand.

Núoro, although not overly endowed with sights, is well worth scratching the surface of to discover some of the island's best museums. It is also a good base for visiting the mural town of Orgosolo and the carnival town, Mamoiada. Nearby, too, is Monte Ortobene and the dramatic range of the Gennargentu. Today the image of mountain bandits is still bolstered by some fanciful tourist literature, but, in reality, new roads and communications have tamed those antisocial scenarios, although sheep rustling continues and doubtless vendettas are still waged, but quietly.

To the east lies the spectacular, undeveloped coastline of the Golfo di Orosei, which is now a national park. Near Dorgali, the Grotta di Ispinigoli has Europe's tallest stalagmite, and on the coast the exceptional bay beaches and caves are the attraction. Cala Gonone on the coast is spectacularly set against an amphitheatre of forested mountains and, although now a popular resort, still has a villagey, laid-back atmosphere. From here there are excellent hiking and climbing excursions, including the Gola Su Gorruppu Gorge and Tiscali, the Nuraghic village, concealed in a mountain chasm.

The mountain range of the Supramonte

Getting Your Bearings

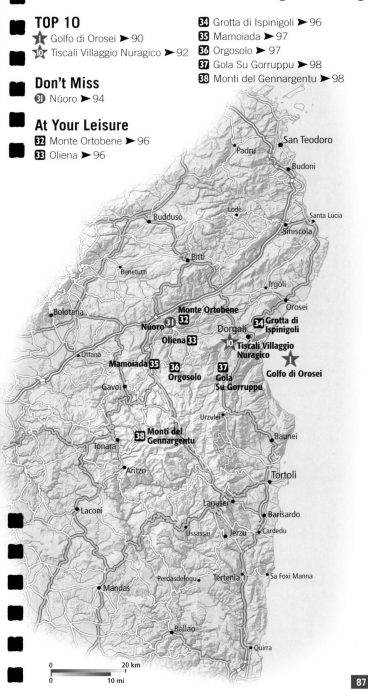

Four Perfect Days

If you're not quite sure where to begin your travels, this itinerary recommends a practical and enjoyable four days exploring Núoro and the East, taking in some of the best places to see. For more information see the main entries (➤ 90–98).

Day 1

Morning
Travel to **31 Núoro** (➤ 94). Head to the old part of town and visit the Museo Deleddiano. Walk to the Corso Garibaldi and have a coffee at **Bar Majore**. Just to the east is the Piazza Santa Maria della Neve, where you can visit the eponymous cathedral.

Lunch
Have lunch at **Il Rifugio** (➤ 100).

Afternoon
Walk south to the outstanding **Museo della Vita e delle Tradizioni Sarde** (of which one of the exhibits is shown in the picture on the left). In the late afternoon, as the sun loses its intensity, drive to **32 Monte Ortobene** (➤ 96) where you can enjoy a panoramic view of the Supramonte mountain range. Located right out in the countryside, the solitary **Hotel Su Gologone** offers an attractive option for accommodation and food – and has earned a reputation for its fine Sardinian dishes. Before you sit down, it is well worth going to admire the gushing water of the Su Gologone natural spring.

Day 2

Morning
Set off for the ⭐**Golfo di Orosei** (➤ 90)! Leave early for Cala Gonone and from there with an excursion boat to **Grotta del Bue Marino** and the dream bay of **Cala Luna** for a swim, before the sun disappears behind the mountains in the early afternoon.

Lunch
Take a break on the inviting terrace of the **Ristorante Ispinigoli** by the car park beneath the caves.

Monte Ortobene
Grotta di Ispinigoli
Núoro **31** **32**
Oliena **33** **34** Golfo di Orosei
10
Mamoiada **35** **36** **37** Orosei
Orgosolo Gola Su Tiscali Villaggio
Gorruppu Nuragico
38
Monti del Gennargentu

Afternoon and Evening

After dinner, visit the **34 Grotta di Ispinigoli** (left; ➤ 96). Then go to the charming little mountain village of Dorgali to do some shopping. Eat and then stay overnight at the **Albergo Sant'Elene** (➤ 100) in the valley of Riu Flumineddu.

Day 3

Morning and afternoon

You will need a backpack for your picnic and hiking boots for today's excursion. Drive along the Flumineddu Valley until the end of the road. From there you set off on foot to **37 Gola Su Gorruppu** (➤ 98). A well-marked path takes you into the Supramonte mountains to the legendary Nuraghic village **Tiscali** (➤ 92; admission fee €5).

Evening

You can book into the Hotel Nuraghe Arvu (➤ 99) in Cala Gonone (below), eat a meal on the terrace high above the sea in and then fall into bed afterwards.

Day 4

Morning

Drive via Oliena to **36 Orgosolo** (➤ 97) and then stroll along at your leisure. Then drive up to the wildly romantic Pratobello. There, you can enjoy a solitary lunch in the restaurant **Ai Monti del Gennargentu** (➤ 101). (You can also stay here overnight.)

Afternoon

Park at the end of the Pratobello road at the Forest Station and wander up the marked path to the striking peak of the 1,316m (4,317ft) high **Monte Novo** (there and back about 2.5 hr). The panorama at the top is sensational! Then make a stop at **35 Mamoiada**, visit the interesting **Museo delle Maschere** (➤ 97) and the mask cutter Ruggero Mameli in his workshop (Via Antonio Crisponi 19) or his impressive private mask museum (Corso Vittorio Emanuele 3).

★Golfo di Orosei

Stretching for 40km (25mi), the Gulf of Orosei has the longest undeveloped coastline in the Mediterranean. Limestone cliffs and rock formations scatter the coastline punctuated by beautiful coves, secluded grottoes and the most glorious hidden beaches.

The gulf is a symmetrical arch extending from Capo Nero in the north to Capo Monte Santo in the south. It is the seafront of the **Supramonte**, a wild and steep coast where holm oak forests, centuries-old juniper trees and *macchia* extend down to the sea. The royal eagle, Eleonora's falcon and griffon vulture are regular residents and these birds of prey can often be seen peeping out from their eyries on the cliff tops.

Excursion boats take visitors out to the wonderful Cala Luna

Orosei Town

Much of the architecture in Orosei town is Spanish, reflecting its former rule by the Aragonese. It's a pleasant place to stroll around, starting at the **Piazza del Popolo**, where you'll find the 13th-century **Cattedrale di San Giácomo** with its 18th-century neoclassical facade and gilded interior. On the west side of town the 15th-century **Sant'Antonio Abate** with its Pisan watchtower is worth a look, although it has been extensively restored.

On the coast, Marina di Orosei has a 6km (3.5mi) quiet stretch of golden sand, framed by pines and lapped by emerald water.

Grotta del Bue Marino

South down the coast, **Cala Gonone** has a gorgeous setting around a harbour framed by soaring mountains. Once a little fishing village, it took off as a tourist resort when the Grotta del Bue Marino opened in the 1950s.

This is the largest and most dramatically beautiful of the many grottoes on this coast. The *bue marino* ("sea ox") is the local name for the monk seal, common a century ago but now one of the world's most endangered mammals. This cave was one of its last hiding places in Sardinia, although the last sightings were back in 1992. A tour takes you to where fresh and saltwater mingle in lakes and the light playing on the water reveals fantastical pink and

**Grotta del
Bue Marino**

white formations in the stalactites and stalagmites. A relief
on the rocky wall at the entrance, showing a dozen dancing
figures around a solar disc, has been verified as graffiti
from the Neolithic period.

Glorious Beaches

Cala Gonone itself has no natural beaches, the ones that
are there are man-made. Other beaches, such as Cala
Fuili, Cala Cartoe and beautiful 🏊 **Cala Luna** are all within a few kilometres. Accessible only by boat, the coves
are surrounded by crystal waters, perfect for swimming
and snorkelling. Boat excursions can be arranged on
the harbour.

TAKING A BREAK

From June to September, the romantic **Bar Su Neulagi**
is open in the Cala Luna, in which guests are served cool
drinks and snacks between the blooming oleander

✚ 173 E3

Grotta del Bue Marino
☎ 0784 93305 ⏰ Weather permitting, visits July 10, 11, noon and 3;
Aug 9, 10, 11, noon, 3, 4 and 5; Sep 10, 11 and 3; Oct, March–June 11 and 3
🎟 €20

INSIDER INFO

It is possible to reach **Cala Luna on foot** from Cala Fuili – by a fairly
precipitous rough track (marked with a red arrow) for around 5km
(3mi). You need good shoes and to be fairly fit; it is steep on the
way up and on the way down. You can always return on one of the
regular boats (tickets at the Su Neulagi bar).

⭐10 Tiscali Villaggio Nuragico

Renato Soru, former President of Sardinia and founder of the Italian internet service provider Tiscali, named his company after an ancient Nuraghic site on the top of Monte Tiscali in the centre of his native Sardinia. The inaugural advertising slogan was "Tiscali. From a land of silence comes a new way of communication."

In the heart of the Supramonte, **Tiscali** houses the remains of a village dating back to the final Nuraghic period. Nearby, the **Gola Su Gorruppu** is one of the deepest and most dramatic canyons in Europe. **Monte Tiscali** stands at 515m (1,690ft) and within it is a wide crater concealing the Nuraghic village – originally a site of more than 60 round dwellings, most now ruined. It is thought that it was built in late Nuraghic times to escape the Roman domination, for which this was a perfect spot given the rugged terrain and high crater walls. The site continued to be inhabited into medieval times, but was only discovered in the 19th century and is still under excavation. It is a very atmospheric place, buried in the mountain with stalactites and trees inside and remnants of the nuraghi within.

The Sa Sedda 'e Sos Carros archaeological site

🔟 Trek to Tiscali
It's best to take a guide to do this full-day trek, organized through the tourist information office in Oliena (▶96). However, should you wish to undertake it on your own (and risk not finding the signs) the best starting point is from the

natural spring at Sorgente Su Gologone next to the Hotel Su Gologone, just off the Oliena–Dorgali road.

From the spring there is a signpost for the **Valle di Lanaittu**, a track that is mainly un-asphalted so best tackled in a 4×4 vehicle or on foot. After about 6km (4mi) you will reach the **rifugio Lanaitho**, a way station with a bar, WC, showers and info point. Here, too, you can obtain tickets for guided tours to the nearby grottoes of Sa Oche, and Su Bentu, and to the Nuraghic holy spring **Sa Sedda 'e Sos Carros**. Walk along the main track past the Grotta Sa Oche keeping left to climb up a steep dirt track. Look for the boulder with painted arrow for Tiscali and follow it to the left up a very steep mule trail until you arrive finally at a wide ledge with superb views over the Valle Lanaittu. After another 30 minutes on foot, keep left on the steepest, over-hanging part of the mountain and take the narrow path to the right over the rocks to the huge *dolina* (cavern) and entrance to Tiscali (€5). In the half-light of the cavern, the deserted village is a spooky but very moving sight.

Monte Tiscali is a dramatic setting for the remains of Tiscali Villaggio Nuragico

TAKING A BREAK

Relax in the abundant shade of the trees at the enchanting hotel bar **Su Gologone** (➤ 101), in which many shepherds and trekking guides meet in the afternoon.

Insider Tip

➕ 173 D3 🕐 May–Sep daily 9–7; Oct–April 9–5; Sa Sedda 'e Sos Carros, Grotta Sa Oche, Grotta Su Bentu: April–Oct daily 9–6
ℹ️ Excursions depart from Dorgali. Coop Ghivine (Via Montebello 5, Dorgali; tel: 0784 96721; www.ghivine.com) has departures at 9am, returning at about 4:30. Price €40, including entrance to Tiscali und Open-Air picnic

Tourist Information
ℹ️ Presidio turistico, Corso Vittorio Emanuele II 72, Oliena
☎️ 0784 286 078 🕐 Jun–Aug Mon–Sat 9–1, 4–7, Sun 9–1

Sa Sedda 'e Sos Carros
✉️ Strada Provinciale 46, Oliena ☎️ 349 508 2766;
www.ilportalesardo.it/archeo/nuoliena.htm 🕐 9:30–6:30 💶 €5

INSIDER INFO

Anyone who would like to dip into the literary world of Sardinia should read the works of the Nobel Prize winner, born in Núoro, **Grazia Deledda** (1871–1936). Her book *canne al vento, (Reeds in the Wind),* for which she won the world's most renowned prize for literature in 1926, is about the hard life of three sisters. The graphic description of human fates and the mythical impression of the isolated mountain region are brought together here in a very readable way.

㉛ Núoro

Núoro, the provincial capital, is at the heartland of Sardinia's traditions and, although not especially aesthetically pleasing, gave birth to distinguished literary sons and daughters whose lives have been indelibly marked by this overgrown mountain village of granite. D H Lawrence followed up his remark that there was nothing to see in Núoro by saying "I am not Baedeker". But then, he wasn't a Nobel Prize winner like writer Grazia Deledda either.

The old part of town in the northeast spreads around Piazza San Giovanni and Corso Garibaldi. On the northern fringes is the **Museo Deleddiano**, the birthplace and home of Grazia Deledda (1871–1936). She was the first Italian woman to win the Nobel Prize for Literature (1926) and is one of Italy's most important early 20th-century "realist" writers. Her writings describe life on her native island with depth and sympathy and deal with human problems in general. She lived here for 29 years and the museum gives an insight into life in a Nuorese house, together with her memorabilia, including first editions, press clippings and her old photos.

The facade of Duomo Santa Maria della Neve

Cathedral
On **Piazza Santa Maria della Neve** is Núoro's neoclassical cathedral. Completed in 1854, it is more quantitative than qualitative. But inside, among the mainly 20th-century paintings, the *Disputa de Gesù Fra i Dottori (Jesus' Dispute in the Temple)* is a 17th-century canvas attributed to the Neapolitan studio of Luca Giordano. Behind the cathedral there are spectacular views out across the valley to Monte Ortobene.

Insider Tip

Museum of Sardinian Life
South of the Duomo is the most famous attraction in Núoro – the **Museo della Vita e delle Tradizioni Sarde** – often referred to simply as the "Museo del Costume".

INSIDER INFO

A highlight for art lovers is the **Museo Ciusa** (Piazza Santa Maria delle Neve; tel: 0784 253 052; www.tribunuoro.it; Tue–Sun 10–1 and 4:30–8:30; admission fee €2), which is housed in an old prison. On show are numerous works by the famous sculptor **Francesco Ciusa** (1893–1949) who was born in Núoro.

There are 7,000 items here, but they may not all be on display, since the museum is undergoing major reorganization. The breathtaking collection of **traditional costumes** will be, however, and they are the highlight, showing the vast variety in styles and the amazingly sophisticated hand needlework produced all across the island. Gorgeous **jewellery** ranges from intricate silver filigree to wild boar tusks. Displays of decorative arts surround the costumes. The other highlight certain to be on view is the display on the *mamuthones* and other carnival costumes and masks from Barbagia (► 16, 97).

Traditional costumes from the early 20th century in the Museum of Sardinian Life

TAKING A BREAK

Have a coffee at the **Bar Majore** (► 100) on Corso Garibaldi 71, which is Núoro's oldest and most opulent café.

✚ 172 C4

Museo Deleddiano
✉ Via Grazia Deledda 43 ☎ 0784 258 088; www.isresardegna.it
🕐 16 March to 30 Sep 9–1, 3–6; 1 Oct to 15 March 10–1, 3–7; closed Mon
🎟 Free

Duomo Santa Maria della Neve
✉ Piazza Santa Maria della Neve 🕐 Daily 8–1, 4–7

Museo della Vita e delle Tradizioni Sarde
✉ Via A Mereu 56 ☎ 0784 257 035
🕐 16 March to 30 Sep Tue–Sun 9–1, 3–6; 1 Oct to 15 March 10–1, 3–5
🎟 €3

At Your Leisure

32 Monte Ortobene

East of Núoro, the road winds up to Monte Ortobene (995m/3,264ft) and its glorious vistas over the valley floor and Supramonte massif. A dusty track leads to 49 steps that climb up to an enormous bronze statue of *Il Redentore (Christ the Redentore)* at 955m (3,130ft). The statue shows Christ trampling the devil underfoot and is a site of great pilgrimage. The *Sagra del Redentore* (➤ 40), Núoro's most important festival, takes place every year in late August, culminating on 29 August, when a long procession is made here from the cathedral.

This is a very popular spot for a picnic in the surrounding woods, and there are a couple of bars and restaurants as well as stalls selling cold drinks and souvenirs.

➕ 172 C4 🚍 No 8 from Piazza Vittorio Emanuele in Núoro (16 June to 16 Sep only)

33 Oliena

Oliena is a lively cosmopolitan town, on the slopes at the foot of Monte Corrasa. Its slate rubble houses and narrow streets still breathe the world of Grazzia Deledda. It is famous for its colourful embroideries, its olive oil and its red Cannonau Nepente di Oliena, regarded as one of the best wines on the island. Not far away is the **Su Gologne** spring.

The pioneers of TrekkingCoop Enis brought this cosmopolitism to the area, and were followed by hikers from all over the world, which is how Oliena developed into a trekking centre.

Insider Tip
Oliena should not be underestimated as a haven of Sardinian cuisine either: its three restaurants, Cikappa, Masiloghi and Sa Corte, have earned it a reputation as a culinary mecca.

➕ 172 C3

34 🏠 Grotta di Ispinigoli

Towering up to 38m (125ft), the central stalagmite of this cave is the tallest in Europe. From the entrance 280 steps lead 60m (200ft) into the grotto. Nine streams flow through these extra-terrestrial surroundings where the temperature remains at a constant 16–17°C (60–62°F).

Estimated to be 180 million years old, but only discovered in 1927, the grotto has yielded some remarkable finds – including fossils dating back to the ice age, bronze and silver bracelets and necklaces. All these items were typically found in Punic burial tombs. Human skeletal remains have also fuelled speculation that this was once a place of human sacrifice.

The **Abisso delle Vergini** (Abyss of the Virgins) is the well that leads into this second cavity, 40m (130ft) below. Theories abound such as the possibility that richly bejewelled young women were sacrificed by throwing them down the well, but it's more probable that it was used as an ancient burial ground. Nearby is the open-air museum **S'Abba Frisca**.

➕ 173 E4

Grotta di Ispinigoli

Grotta di Ispinigoli
✉ Just off the Orosei–Dorgali road
☎ 078 496 2431 🕐 June 10–5; July, Aug 10–6; April, May, Sep, Oct 10–noon, 3–5; Nov, Dec 11–noon. Tours depart on the hour 💶 €7

S'Abba Frisca
ℹ www.sabbafrisca.com 💶 €7.50

35 🎭 Mamoiada

Every year at carnival time Mamoiada erupts into a frenzy of shaggy sheep-skinned men wearing demonic black wooden masks and weighed down by heavy cowbells. These traditional costumed figures, known as *mamuthones*, have pagan origins, and this ritual is an attempt to drive out demons of winter. They shuffle along, rattling cowbells behind their backs; they represent defeated men and animals and are subjugated by the *issokadores* – men dressed in red and white wielding lassos. The **Museo delle Maschere Mediterranee** (Tue–Sun 9–1, 3–7) contains examples of these costumes and others from the Mediterranean basin. These demonstrate the similarities and commonality among the masks and carnival celebrations of various cultures in the region, including the Alps, Spain and the Balkans. Ruggero Mameli, one of the last and best mask carvers, lives and works in Mamoiada. Visit his impressive private mask museum and then his atelier, where you can also buy masks made using the traditional method.
➕ 172 C3

Museo delle Maschere Mediterranee
✉ Piazza Europa 15
☎ 0784 569 018; www.museodellemaschere.it
🕐 Tue–Sun 10–1, 3–6 💶 €4

Mameli Workshop
✉ Via Antonio Crisponi 19
☎ 0784 56222; www.mascheremameli.com

Museo Mameli
✉ Corso Vittorio Emanuele 3

Getting away from it all on a hiking holiday in Sardinia

36 Orgosolo

A painted rock depicting "the landowner of Orgosolo" greets you outside the entrance to this town of murals. The figure, often erroneously referred to as the "fat, greedy landowner" actually shows a shepherd looking out for his herd on the horizon. The history of Murales in Orgosolo began in 1968 with the first mural by the Milanese anarchist group Dioniso, which depicted a map of Italy putting a large question mark in the place of Sardinia. This encourages the art teacher Francesco del Casino, together with his students, to paint other walls with political and satirical motifs. Nowadays, many are devoted to modern-day as well as political themes – from folkloric figures, to the destruction of New York's Trade Center on 11 September 2001. The *Festa dell'Assunta* takes place in Orgosolo on 15 August – a highlight of Barbagia and one of the top processions of the region.
➕ 172 C3

Núoro & the East

37 Gola Su Gorruppu

This is one of Europe's most spectacular gorges, carved out of limestone by the river Flumineddu, with cliffs soaring to more than 400m (1,300ft). The colour of the limestone and microclimate within make this an unforgettable experience. The entire length of the gorge is some 8km (5mi) but you need proper equipment and a guide to venture a long way inside.

By car from Dorgali, take the lower bypass to the west (SS125) then follow the signpost for the Sant' Elene Hotel. From the hotel, it is another 4km (2.5mi) drive on a single-lane tarred road to a bridge where you can park the car. It is about a two-hour trek to the gorge from here.

➕ 173 D3

Cooperativa Gorropu
✉ Passo Silana SS125, Km 183, Urzulei
☎ 333 850 7157; www.gorropu.com

38 Monti del Gennargentu

Meaning "silver gate", the Gennargentu is the highest massif in Sardinia and in winter the wild mountain terrain of the Parco del Gennargentu is covered in snow. There are many villages dotted around; none are especially attractive, but they make good walking bases. Sardinia's highest village is Fonni, lying at 1,000m (3,280ft) above sea level. The highest peaks are all accessible from here: Bruncu Spina at 1,829m (6,000ft) and Punta La Marmora at 1,834m (6,016ft). The strenuous climb to the top of Punta La Marmora is rewarded with fabulous views over the entire island. For a less demanding foray, it's possible to drive most of the way up to Bruncu Spina to the valley station of the ski lift at 1,500m (4,920ft), from where it's a relatively easy hike to the top.

The area is thickly vegetated with holm oak and chestnut woods. The lower flanks are cloaked in vineyards that produce the famous red wine made from the Cannonau grape, and this area is also especially noted for its pecorino cheese.

➕ 172 B1/2

Enjoying a day out in the Gennargentu mountains

Where to...
Stay

Prices
Expect to pay for a double room per night:
€ under €90   **€€** €90–€155   **€€€** €155–€250   **€€€€** over €250

GOLFO DI OROSEI

Hotel Costa Dorada €€–€€€
This charming hotel has 28 comfortable rooms decorated in traditional style and a vine-shaded dining terrace with views over the Gulf of Orosei. In season, it has exclusive use of *The Marlin* – a 55-foot boat (extra cost) to reach hidden coves and beaches.

Insider Tip

➕ 173 E3
✉ Lungomare Palmasera 45, Cala Gonone
☎ 0784 93332; www.hotelcostadorada.it
🕓 Apr–Oct

Hotel Nuraghe Arvu €€–€€€
Perched high above the sea, this beautiful complex has a wonderful view. Grouped around the pool are one-storey buildings designed in Sardinian-Moorish style that provide a total of 50 tastefully appointed and spacious rooms and suites (three are suitable for disabled guests). All of the rooms have a terrace or balcony. A small oasis just 800m from the centre – and yet far away from the hustle and bustle.

Insider Tip

➕ 173 E3 ✉ Viale Bue Marino, Cala Gonone
☎ 0784 920 075; www.hotelnuraghearvu.com
🕓 15 April to 15 Oct

Hotel Il Querceto €€–€€€
On the southwestern side of the town, this three-star property is in the typical mountain style. Rooms are airy and all overlook woodland from their balconies. The attractive gardens also have tennis courts.

➕ 173 D3 ✉ Via Lamarmora 4, Dorgali
☎ 0784 96509; www.ilquerceto.com 🕓 All year

Hotel Su Barchile €€
This very welcoming three-star hotel has 10 rooms housed in a former dairy. It is modern and very comfortable and all 10 rooms are air-conditioned. It also has a highly regarded restaurant (➤ 100).

➕ 173 E4 ✉ Via Mannu 5, Orosei
☎ 0784 98879; www.subarchile.it

OLIENA

Hotel Su Gologone €€€–€€€€
Located 7km (4mi) east of Oliena near the Su Gologone spring in park-like grounds at the foot of the Supramonte, this is one of Sardinia's loveliest hotels. The complex is a treasure chest of Sardinian art, the cuisine in the first-class restaurant absolutely authentic. There are 68 stylishly furnished rooms as well as a beauty and wellness centre. In addition, the hotel offers excursions to the Supramonte, either on horseback or in a jeep.

➕ 172 C3 ✉ Località Su Gologone
☎ 0784 287 512; www.sugologone.it
🕓 April to 15 Dec

B&B Santa Maria €
Centrally located near the church, this well-kept B&B is housed in a historical building. It offers six invitingly furnished rooms with modern bathrooms, a large, partially covered terrace with an open kitchen, sun chairs and a view over the roofs of the Old Town to Cedrino Valley.

➕ 172 C3 ✉ Piazza Santa Maria, corner of Via Grazia Deledda 76 ☎ 0784 287 278;
www.bbsantamaria.it 🕓 March–Nov

Where to...
Eat and Drink

Prices
Expect to pay per person for a meal, excluding drinks:
€ under €26   €€ €26–€55   €€€ over €55

NÚORO

Bar Majore/Caffè Tettamanzi €
Something of an institution, this is Núoro's oldest café. The opulent interior has a frescoed ceiling, gilded stucco and antiques. It's a great place for immersing yourself in the local atmosphere.
➕ 172 C4 ✉ Corso Garibaldi 71
🕐 Daily lunch and dinner; closed Sun

Il Rifugio €–€€
Close to Madonna delle Grazie, this bustling trattoria/pizzeria is very popular with the locals. Pasta and pizza are specialities, and you can watch the pizzas being made.
➕ 172 C4 ✉ Via Antonio Mereu 28/36
☎ 0784 232 355; www.trattoriarifugio.com
🕐 Thu–Tue; closed Oct, Nov

Ristorante Grillo €–€€
The chef at this popular, award-winning in-town restaurant values fresh local vegetables, featuring them in original seasonal dishes. Don't miss the pasta, which is made on the premises.
➕ 172 C4 ✉ Via Monsignor Melas 1
☎ 0784 38668 🕐 Daily lunch and dinner

GOLFO DI OROSEI

Colibrì €–€€
This warm, welcoming, family-run restaurant specializes in traditional Sardinian cuisine such as *cinghiale* (wild boar) and *porceddu* (suckling pig). It also has good fish dishes.
➕ 173 D3 ✉ Via Gramsci 14 (corner of Via Floris), Dorgali ☎ 0784 96054
🕐 July, Aug daily; March–Oct Mon–Sat

Costa Dorada €€
The vine-shaded terrace restaurant of this pretty, family-run hotel overlooks the Gulf of Orosei. On offer are fresh catch of the day fish specials as well as meat, all inspired by traditional Sard recipes.
➕ 173 E3 ✉ Lungomare Palmasera 45, Cala Gonone ☎ 0784 493 332 🕐 Apr–Oct

Ristorante Albergo Sant'Elene €–€€
Lying 3km (1.5mi) off the SS125 from Dorgali, this restaurant is perched on a hillside. From the terrace there are glorious views, and the typical regional cuisine is no less splendid. Roast suckling pig, lamb, fish and appetizers of home-made pâté are complemented by good wine and friendly service. There are also excellent pizzas.
➕ 173 D3 ✉ Località Sant'Elene, Dorgali
☎ 0784 94572; www.hotelsantelene.net
🕐 Summer daily; winter Tue–Sun; closed Jan

Ristorante Al Porto €€
Feast on local delicacies in the locals' favourite restaurant overlooking the port. Host Simone Spanu, affectionately known as Pop, is infectious in his enthusiasm for seafood – fishermen advise him of the catch of the day. Try "Sardinian caviar" *(bottarga)*, here served to perfection with spaghetti.
➕ 173 E3 ✉ Hotel Pop, Piazza del Porto 2, Cala Gonone ☎ 0784 93185; www.hotelpop.it
🕐 Daily lunch and dinner

Su Barchile €€–€€€
This very good restaurant prides itself on the traditions of the sea and

land combined in natural flavours. Gourmets love dishes like *porcetto* with myrtle or the 44 fish and seafood variations. Try the delicious puddings served with the establishment's own *moscato* (muscat). The outdoor terrace is perfect for summer dining.

➕ 173 E4 ✉ Via Mannu 5, Orosei
☎ 0784 98879; www.subarchile.it
🕐 Daily lunch and dinner

Trattoria S'Hostera €€

The no frills ambience: white walls, tiled floor and simple seating is offset by Maurizio's great food. There is only one daily menu (with starters, pasta, fish and meat dishes) – and everything is guaranteed to be absolutely fresh.

➕ 173 E4 ✉ Via G. Deledda 56, Orosei
☎ 380 701 4355
🕐 Mon–Fri lunch and dinner, Sat lunch only

OLIENA

Ristorante Masiloghi €€

Small, charming restaurant with excellent regional cuisine served in the stylish dining room. Specials include *maccarrones a bocciu* (Sardinian gnocchi), *malloreddus* (ravioli stuffed with sheep cheese or ricotta) or *pane frattau*, the Sard pizza. Many products are locally produced, such as the light and sweet red wine Su Durdurinu, olive oil, honey and the *pane carasau*.

➕ 172 C3 ✉ Via Galiani 68, Oliena
☎ 0784 285 696; www.masiloghi.it
🕐 Daily lunch and dinner

Su Gologone €€€

This legendary restaurant, run – since it was promoted from being a roadside barbecue hut – by the Palimodde family, is a haven for authentic, top quality Sardinian food. Eating and staying at Su Gologone (►99) is a real and unforgettable highlight.

➕ 172 C3 ✉ Hotel Su Gologone, Località Su Gologone ☎ 0784 287 512; www.sugologone.it
🕐 Daily lunch and dinner, by reservation

GROTTA DI ISPINIGOLI

Hotel/Ristorante Ispinigoli €–€€

Below the grotto entrance, the panoramic restaurant terrace is a good place to relax while waiting for a tour of the grotto. With set menus for vegetarians, fish, seafood and meat options as well as an à la carte menu. Incredible selection of 600 different wines.

➕ 173 E4
✉ Grotta di Ispinigoli
☎ 0784 95268; www.hotelispinigoli.com
🕐 April–Oct daily lunch and dinner

ORGOSOLO

Il Portico €

Simple, authentic and traditional fare in the mountain village's historical centre. The accommodating owners also organise meals with shepherds al fresco, Murales tours and tips for treks and excursions. *Insider Tip*

➕ 172 C3 BVia Giovanni XXIII 34, Orgosolo
☎ 0784 402 929, www.ristoranteorgosolo.it
🕐 All year; closed Sun

Ristorante/Hotel Ai Monti del Gennargentu €€

This solitary, rustic restaurant, located about 5km (3mi) outside of Pratobello under old oak trees serves authentic Barbagia dishes: lamb, goat and boar, handmade pasta, hearty soups and fresh vegetables. Hotel rooms are also available.

➕ 172 C3 ✉ Località Settiles
☎ 0784 402 374 🕐 Daily lunch and dinner

Where to...
Shop

NÚORO

In Núoro there is an **ISOLA** outlet (►43) for authentic handmade

crafts at Via Bua Monsignore 10
(tel: 0784 31507; Mon–Sat 9–1,
4–8). For gourmet delicacies visit
pasticceria **L'Oasi Deliciosa** at Via
Sardegna 37. Specialities include
aranzada di Núoro (candied orange
peel and almonds).

DORGALI & OLIENA

The little village towns of Dorgali
and Oliena are renowned for their
craftsmanship. Here, you will find
woven goods, knives, ceramics and
leather. A good address for hand-
woven work is **Angelina Carta** (Via
Lamarmora 128). **Luciano Spanu**
(Via G. Deledda 17) sells traditional
Sardinian shepherds' knives, Dorgali
near **Canzittu** (Via Lamarmora 76)
is the place for leather ware, as is
Calzoleria/Pelletteria Corrias (Via
G. B. Melis 10) in Oliena. You can
get pecorino in Dorgali at the sheep
farm **cooperative Coop Dorgali Pastori**
(Loc. Golloi, www.dorgalipastori.it).
Cannonau can be bought at **Cantina
Sociale** (Via Piemonte 11, www.
cantinadorgali.it), and Nepente di
Oliena is on sale in Oliena at the
Cantina Sociale (Via Núoro 1, www.
cantinasocialeoliena.it).

Where to...
Go Out

ACTIVITIES

The area around Núoro is very
scenic, hilly and untamed. The
mountains around Oliena are full
of grottoes and passageways where
there are superb opportunities for
climbing and canyoning. Two
cooperatives offer hikes, walks,
rock climbing and cave- and
canyon-exploration trips by reservation in the Gulf of Orosei and
Gennargentu region: **Cooperativa**

Ghivine (Via Lamarmora 69e,
Dorgali; tel: 0784 96721; www.
ghivine.com) and **Cooperativa
Gorropu** (Passo Silana, at the top
of the pass on SS125, Km 183,
Urzulei; tel: 333 850 7157; www.
gorropu.com).

For quad biking or cross-country
driving, contact **Barbagia Insolita**
(Corso Vittorio Emanuele 48,
Oliena; tel: 0784 286 005; www.
barbagiainsolita.it).

If you want to explore the coast
alone, rent a **motorboat** in Cala
Gonone from one of the companies
with kiosks on the harbour front.

Cala Gonone is also a good
centre for **diving** and there are
several clubs such as the Argonauta,
Via dei Lecci 10 (tel: 0784 93046;
www.argonauta.it). On offer are
guided snorkelling tours accompanied by professional guides;
dives on World War II wrecks and
caverns.

NIGHTLIFE

This part of the island soon shows
its limitations in terms of nightlife.
Núoro is the only place with clubs
and discos that are open all year
round. These include the disco
KillTime (Via Mereu 45) and the
Latino club **La Boca Chica** (Via
Mughina 94). Live music is avail-
able at **La Grotta Dei Poeti** (Via
Marconi 7).

In the coastal regions, the clubs
and discos are only open during
the season. You can dance away
the night in the disco-club **Long
Coast Bay** in Cala Gonone (Spiaggia
di Palmasera) or in Oasi in Orosei
(Via Nazionale 161). Blues music
to unwind can be enjoyed at the
Roadhouse Pub in Cala Gonone
(Lungomare Palmasera 28), cocktails, drinks and live music are
served at the harbour in **Su Recreu**
(Piazza Andrea Doria). In Orosei
in-bar **Yesterday** pulls in the night
owls with its live music (Via
Nazionale 48).

Sássari &
the Northwest

 **Little Treats**

The best Ice Cream in Alghero
Gelateria I Bastione serves the best ice cream in town; its own "laboratory" produces the mouth-watering creations (► 110).

Malvasia di Bosa
At the *enoteca* **run by the Columbu family** in Bosa, the Malvasia is served with cheese, olives and bread, which makes it taste even better (► 124).

Watch Out for the Vultures
From the car park at Capo Marargiu on the coastal road from Alghero to Bosa, you can see **griffon vultures** circling overhead (► 120).

Getting Your Bearings

Sardinia's northwest is very diverse. The tourist hotspot is bubbly Alghero and Capo Cáccia, while Bosa, the little town, along the banks of the Temo river offers a quieter ambience. The area's urban centre is Sássari, Sardinia's second largest town. One of the most beautiful beaches can be found in the remote Stintino, where boats take visitors over to the island of Asinara. Impressive evidence of the Nuraghic culture awaits you inland with culturally and historically significant sacral structures along "The Way of the Churches".

The Parco Nazionale dell'Asinara, a nature reserve on the island of the same name, is home to rare miniature albino donkeys and ringed by glorious white beaches that meld into turquoise waters. The jumping-off point for the island is the little seaside resort of Stintino, with the breathtakingly beautiful beach Spiaggia della Pelosa. The neighbouring harbour town of Porto Torres is an attractive excursion destination with some excellent sights such as the magnificent Basilika San Gavino. The Carlo Felice highway provides a connection to Sássari, a town still off the main tourist routes. This lively university and commercial town has an attractive old centre with winding streets and small shops, studios, cafés and bars.

The marina in Alghero

Alghero attracts thousands of visitors with its beautiful beaches and its charming Spanish-Catalan architecture strewn along a medieval maze of alleyways. Excursion boats set off from the harbour for Grotta di Nettuno on Capo Cáccia. The road along the wildly romantic, uninhabited coast between Alghero and Bosa, where griffon vultures nest, is one of the most beautiful coastal routes on the island. Inland, you can see the Nuraghe Su Antine in Valle dei Nuraghi, visit the spectacular cave graves of Sant Andria Priu near Bonorva, or Sa Coveccada, the most impressive megalithic tomb in the Mediterranean region.

Getting Your Bearings

TOP 10

At Your Leisure

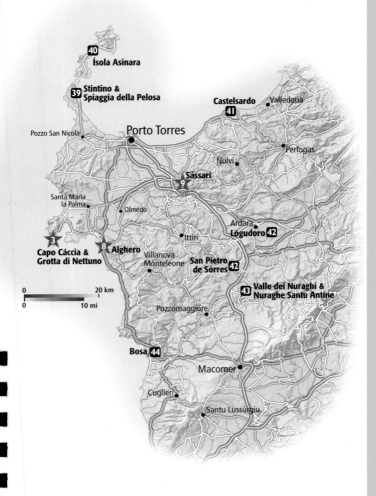

Perfect Days in...

Three Perfect Days

If you're not quite sure where to begin your travels, this itinerary recommends a practical and enjoyable three days exploring Sássari and the northwest of the island, taking in some of the best places to see. For more information see the main entries (➤ 108–120).

Day 1

Morning
⭐**Sássari** (➤ 112) and its Old Town invite you to enjoy the town's pulsating Mediterranean lifestyle as you wander round and shop. Since there are not many outstanding sights, you can enjoy just soaking up the atmosphere. The most important architectural structure is the baroque Duomo on the eponymous piazza. For the Sassarese, the Santa Maria di Betlem church is just as important the Duomo, because it houses the *candelieri*, the huge candlesticks, which are carried through the streets during the famous procession for the "festival of the candle holders". After drinking a fortifying coffee in the **Florian** (➤ 114) in the Via Roma, you should definitely wander round the New Town districts and look at the stores.

Lunch
In order to try Sássari's speciality *faine* (a sort of pizza made with chickpea flower), it is necessary to go back into the Old Town to **Da Benito** (Via Sant' Apollinare 37), because the *faine* served there are the best in the entire town.

Afternoon
Drive to ⭐**Alghero** (➤ 110) and have a siesta on the long beach (ideally on the Spiaggia Maria Pia). Then stroll through the streets and at sunset go to

the town wall to the **Buena Vista Bar**
(► 122), to watch the sun go down
behind the Capo Cácchia. A good choice
for dinner is **Trattoria Caragol** (► 123),
and for the night **Hotel Angedras** (► 121).

Day 2

Morning
Drive from Alghero along the Riviera del
Corallo past the curious town of Fertilia and
the Le Bombarde and Lazaretto beaches,
until you get to the lovely Porto Conte
bay. After visiting the ★**Grotta di Nettuno**
(► 108) continue via Palmadula and
Pozzo San Nicola to **39 Stintino** (► 116).

Lunch
After stopping for a swim at Pelosa-Strand, savour the view of the island
Asinara from the **I Ginepri** bar that boasts an idyllic location in the sand
dunes.

Afternoon
Then it is off along the coast to Porto Torres in the little coastal town of
41 Castelsardo (► 116). Walk to the Castello there. The Hotel **Baga Baga**
(► 123) is a good place to eat dinner and stay overnight. It is about half a
mile outside the town.

Day 3

Morning
Drive through the mountains to Borutta to the **42 San Pietro de Sórres**
monastery (► 117) and to Dolmen Sa Coveccada by Mores. Then continue along Valle di Nuraghi to **43 Nuraghe Santu Antine** (► 117). From
there it is not far to the Necropolis of Sant'Andria Priu.

Lunch
Fortify yourself with lunch at the
Su Lumarzu restaurant in the
"ghost village" Rebeccu
(7km/4.5mi from Bonorva).

Afternoon
Back on the coast in the
picturesque little town of
44 Bosa (► 120), it is
well worth wandering
along the narrow streets
to Castello. You can take
a break at the **Hotel
Palazzo Sa Pischedda**
(► 121).

⭐ Capo Cáccia & Grotta di Nettuno

One of the top sights on the island is just to the west of Alghero. The limestone rock of the Capo Cáccia promontory has been buffeted and sculpted by wave and wind for 135 million years. From the lookout point there are glorious views over the cape and Ísola Foradada, while around the headland is the spectacular, giddying Escala del Cabirol (literally "goat's steps" in Catalan). This 654-step descent leads to the famous Grotta di Nettuno.

The stunning deep cavern with a lake is known as **Neptune's Grotto**, the mythical abode of nymphs. It is filled with **stalactites and stalagmites** twisted into fantastical shapes – a subterranean fairyland populated by shapes resembling human beings, statues, trees and animals. All is bathed in colour ranging from greenish-blue to white, yellow and orange crystals from the shimmering phosphorescence of the rock.

A tour of the Grotto takes you 200m around the shores of a saltwater lake, **Lamarmora**, facing the Acquasantiera – or holy water font – a huge 2m-high (6.5ft) stalagmite. As the natural light ends and the darkness begins, shapes such as the Great Organ eerily seem to come to life. Guides fondly remember when visitors could row across the lake, lit by thousands of small candles on little plates floated on the water, creating an otherworldly glow of enchantment in the grand chamber. Let your imagination run free with the enchanting spectacle of those tiny, quivering flames throwing shadows on the wall and the reflections in the still waters of the lake.

Getting There
There are two ways to reach the grotto from Alghero. By sea, a

Grotta di Nettuno with its limestone formations

🚢 **boat trip** from the town port takes about an hour to get there. You pass by the Cape Galera and Punto Giglio cliffs, then round the tip of Capo Cáccia to arrive at the mouth of the caves lying at the foot of a towering cliff – a hugely impressive sight.

Overland by car, the caves are 24km (15mi) from Alghero. The **panoramic road** (SS127) curves around Capo Cáccia, unfurling one of Sardinia's best views, taking in the bay of Porto Conte, Alghero itself, and stretching as far south as the Bosa coastline. There is a car park at Capo Cáccia.

TAKING A BREAK

At the top of the steps leading down to the Grotta di Nettuno there is a **bar** serving refreshing drinks and ice creams.

Opposite: Steps down to the cave cling to the sheer cliff face

🚩 166 A2 ✉ Capo Cáccia ☎ 079 946 540 🎧 Guided tours (45 min.) April–Oct daily 9–7; Nov–March daily 10–3, only when the sea is calm 🚢 FROM ALGHERO: Linea Grotte Navisarda; tel: 079 950 603; www.navisarda.it; €16 (without the caves); Linea Grotte Attilio Regolo; tel: 368 353 6824; www.grottedinettuno.it; €15 (without the caves)

INSIDER INFO

Anyone who has problems walking or is not 100% fit should avoid going down the 654 steep steps of the **Escala del Cabirol** to the caves! Those wishing to take this route are best advised to do so in the morning, because from early afternoon, the sun shines mercilessly into the plummeting cliff walls and makes the climb back up to the car park a sweaty ordeal!

Insider Tip

Alghero

The picturesque medieval city is beautifully positioned amid white beaches, on Sardinia's "Riviera del Corallo". Bathed in a warm pink glow, it sits on a small peninsula surrounded by towers and fortifications. In this tourist town and fishing port the lovely old centre has a tangle of narrow lanes filled with bars, restaurants and shops. It also has a distinct Catalan character as a result of Spanish colonization in the 14th century.

Exploring the Old Town

The best place to start is at the excellent tourist information centre (➤ 33) in Piazza Porta Terra, the old main entrance to the city. Looming over the piazza, on which the Algherese like to meet, is **Torre di Porta Terra**. Near by is the majolica dome of the **Chiesa di San Michele**.

The stone streets of the old city, narrow and lined with shops and cafès, are often bridged by arches, and are dotted randomly by small squares. The "main" street of the Old Town is narrow Via Carlo Alberto.

San Michele dominates the skyline with its glistening ceramic dome and is perhaps the most opulent of the baroque churches on the island. The interior is full of sumptuous stucco and fine altar paintings. **San Francesco**, with its stately, pointed Aragonese tower, hosts summer evening concerts.

Alghero's **Cattedrale** interior is a mixture of architectural styles, but the impressive dome dates from the 18th century.

Bastioni (walls) encircle the waterfront

The Waterfront

The waterfront is girded by the *bastoni* (walls), and a walk along here makes a perfect evening *passeggiata*, when the sun descends in a red glow behind the Capo Cáccia. Then people like to meet in the bar Buena Vista Sunset Club. Those who don't find a seat just take their *aperitivo* on the wall.

Insider Tip

TAKING A BREAK

Have a snack at **Focacceria Milese** (➤ 123) on the harbour promenade, there you can also get *foccace*.

✚ 166 B2

Tourist Information Office
✉ Piazza Porta Terra 9
☎ 079 979 054;
www.alghero-turismo.it

Parts of the cloister in Chiesa di San Francesco date back to the 13th century

Chiesa di San Michele
✉ Largo S. Francesco
🕒 Daily from 30 minutes before Mass. Mass: Mon–Fri 10, Sat 10, 7, Sun 9, 7

Chiesa di San Francesco
✉ Via Carlo Alberto, 46
🕒 Mon–Sat 9:15–12:30, 5–6:30, Tue–Fri 4:30–6:30, Sun 9:15am–10:30am

Cattedrale di Santa Maria
✉ Piazza Duomo
🕒 Daily 7–8; tower: June, Sep, Oct Mon, Tue, Thu, Fri, Sat 10:30–1, 7–9:30; July 10:30–1, 7–9:30; Aug Mon, Tue, Thu, Fri, Sat 10.30–1
💶 Free; tower: €2.50

INSIDER INFO

About 9km (5.5mi) north of Alghero, **Necropoli di Anghelu Ruju** (April–Oct daily 9–7; Nov–Feb 10–2; March 9:30–4; entry fee €3) is one of Sardinia's most important ancient sites. The rock tombs are located in the grounds of **Sella & Mosca Vineyard** (tel: 079 997 719; www.sellaemosca.it; Mon–Sat 8:30–5:30; June–Sep until 8; Aug also Sun 9–1, 4–8; guided tours: June–Sep Mon–Sat at 5:30 or by appointment), which produces some of the best wine on the island.

 Sássari

After Cagliari, this is Sardinia's second city – although the Sassarese will tell you that it is the first. It is sophisticated, cheerful, has a thriving café scene and a fascinating *centro storico*, or historical centre. National politicians, including Antonio Segni, Francesco Cossiga and Enrico Berlinguer, have been nurtured here in this, Sardinia's oldest university town.

The Medieval Town

At the core of the *centro storico*, the 15th-century **Duomo di San Nicola** has a baroque fantasy facade, added in the 18th century and very reminiscent of Puglian baroque you can see in Lecce in the south of Italy. The interior is by comparison very bare, although it does contain some works of art, such as the *Madonna con Bambino* by a 16th-century Sardinian artist, which adorns the high altar, and walnut choir stalls.

Around here the lively narrow streets of the old medieval town are perfect for a stroll. Inevitably you will end up at the **Corso Vittorio Emanuele II**. This street is full of *palazzi*, gorgeous wrought-iron balconies and handsome buildings – all in different states of neglect or, more recently, restoration. The lovely Liberty-style **Teatro Cívico** has been beautifully restored and its jewel-box interior is like a miniature version of Milan's La Scala.

The elaborate facade of Duomo di San Nicola

North of here, along Corso Trinità, are remnants of the city's **medieval walls,** while the nearby **Fontana di Rosello** is a splendid Renaissance fountain sculpted in marble and dark stone. At each side there are statues of the four seasons with four white dolphin mouth spouts and eight lion-head spouts.

At Piazza di Santa Maria, close to the site of the original city walls, is the **Chiesa di Santa Maria di Betlem**. Founded in 1106, it has a lovely Romanesque facade, while the inside is more overblown baroque. The lateral chapels display the *candelieri* (giant wooden candles) that represent the town's medieval craft guilds and are paraded for the big 14 August festival, on the evening before Assumption, *I Candelieri* (► 17, 44). Made from wood and polychrome, they are around 4m (13ft) in height and weigh 310kg (685lb).

INSIDER INFO

The **Museo Nazionale G. A. Sanna** (Via Roma 64; tel: 079 272 203, www.museosanna sassari.beniculturali.it, Tue–Sun 9–8; entry fee €4) is next to the National Archaeological Museum, Sardinia's most important archaeological museum. Adjacent to it is the Pinakothek with works by Sardinian artists and an ethnographical collection. A museum offering shopping possibilities for the incredibly diverse Sardinian handicraft is the **Pavillon** located in the middle of the green Giardino Púbblico (municipal part).

Insider Tip

Around Piazza Italia

All roads lead to the heart of town on the **Piazza Italia**. But a stroll along the **Via Roma** just off the piazza is always a delight, as this is the centre of Sássari's thriving café life.

Insider Tip

TAKING A BREAK

Enjoy a drink at **Florian** (➤ 122), just off Piazza d'Italia.

➕ 166 C/D3

Palazzo della Provincia on Piazza Italia, Sássari's grandest square

Duomo di San Nicola
✉ Piazza Duomo
🕐 Daily 8–4:30 ✋ Free

Chiesa di Santa Maria di Betlem
✉ Piazza di Santa Maria
🕐 Daily 8–noon, 4:30–7 ✋ Free

Of Sacred Buildings and Cows

The Santíssima Trinità di Saccargia (Basilica of the Holy Trinity of Saccargia) (▶ 117) rises majestically from a valley basin in the Logudoro region. Its black and white masonry, which reveals a Tuscan influence, is simple yet impressive. If one believes the legend, a cow once kneeled here to pray. This may have inspired the church's name of "sa acca argia" (the spotted cow).

❶ **Bell tower:** Pilasters (vertical, slightly raised architectural elements that look like columns) visibly articulate the height of the square tower, which is 41m (134ft) high, 8m (26ft) long and 8m (26ft) wide.

❷ **Portico:** In addition to the traditional plant motifs, animals and monstrous creatures adorn the capitals and rounded arch of the porch. The cows peacefully resting on the left cornerstone resemble the animal depictions above the founding inscription (1174) on the Leaning Tower of Pisa and probably reference the name of the church: although while "sa acca argia" means "the spotted cow", the name could also be derived from "sa accargia", which means "cowgirl". This church portico is one of a kind in Sardinia.

❸ **Façade:** Two rows of arches decorate the façade. Colourfully designed rosettes are carved into them. There is a cross-shaped opening in the central arch.

❹ **Interior:** The wooden-beamed interior of the single-nave church displays a refined simplicity. It was built after the apse of 1116.

❺ **Frescoes:** One of Sardinia's unique highlights are the Byzantine frescoes in the central apse (13th century). They were probably created by a Pisan artist and among the few remaining works of Romanesque fresco painting in Italy.

Colourful accents have been added to the rosettes on the facade

It is precisely the simplicity of
the interior that makes it so
impressive

At Your Leisure

Boats in the harbour at Stintino waiting for their next trip to the sea

and a picturesque Saracen tower. Absolutely awesome!

➕ 166 B4

40 Ísola Asinara

In 1997 Italy's "Alcatraz", the high-security prison island Asinara, was declared a national park (www.parcoasinara.org). The island takes its name from the white donkeys that live there. There are boat trips which include a tour of the former prison complex. A small train and bus provide transport on the island, and in Fornelli harbour there is a bike rental company. A bar and restaurant in the Cala Reale serve meals, and accommodation is available in the no-frills Ostello Cala d'Oliva (www.sognasinara.it).

➕ 166 B5

41 Castelsardo

The medieval citadel of Castelsardo perches on a rocky outcrop with a jumble of houses at its feet. Known in the 12th century as Castelgenovese, by the mid-15th century it had become Castelaragonese; its strategic importance has long since disappeared but it is still a popular landmark. The main sights are in the Old Town up the steep steps and streets where the Cattedrale di Sant'Antonio Abate is worth a look. From the top of the castle there are splendid views – right across to Corsica, on a clear day. *Insider Tip* The town is known for its handicrafts, especially *l'intreccio* (straw-weaving) – there's a museum devoted to it in the castle.

➕ 167 D4

39 🏃 Stintino & Spiaggia della Pelosa

The friendly little fishing town **Stintino** lies on a peninsula between two bays. Colourful little fishing boats bob up and down on the water, inviting bars, cafés and restaurants line the roads. Excursion boats leave from Stintino for Ísola Asinara.

The famous **Spiaggia della Pelosa** is located several kilometres away. *Insider Tip* La Pelosa, literally "the hairy", is one of Sardinia's most enchanting beaches and because of this paradisiacal beauty is often used as the setting for advertising campaigns. Real South Seas flair – with golden yellow, very gently sloping beach (super for children), the incredible colour of the water

Cattedrale di Sant'Antonio Abate
🕐 June–Sep daily 10–1, 6–midnight 🎫 €3

Museo dell' Intreccio Mediterraneo
✉ Via Marconi ☎ 079 470 220 🕐 June–Sep 9–1, 2–midnight; Oct–May 9:30–1, 3–5:30 🎫 €3

42 Logudoro & San Pietro de Sórres

The Logudoro (literally "place of gold") south and east of Sássari is lovely, rolling countryside, dotted with Romanesque churches left by the Pisans; the SS597, branching off towards Ólbia, is known as the "Way of the Churches". About 16km (10mi) southeast of Sássari, the 12th-century **Basilica della SS Trinità di Saccargia** dominates the countryside – a near-perfect example of Pisan Romanesque style (▶ 114). Dark volcanic basalt contrasts with light limestone stripes and its campanile soars 40m (130ft) high. Other churches line the route, then some 16km (10mi) farther east, perched majestically on a rocky outcrop, you come to **Sant' Antíoco di Bisarcio**. Dating from the 11th century and combining both Pisan and French influences, it is still grandiose although its campanile – built like a castle keep – has been gravely damaged. It is particularly stunning in the late afternoon when the sun is so low that it makes the church glow.

Just a couple of miles further down the road is the black cathedral in Ardara (**Santa Maria del Regno**)

Castelsardo and the medieval castle

with its spectacular high altar, regarded as one of the most awe-inspiring and important churches in Sardinia.

The church tour ends on a hill not far from Borutta with another jewel of Pisan church architecture: the church belonging to the Benedictine monastery **San Pietro di Sórres** with its striped white limestone and black trachyte facade.

Basilica della SS Trinità di Saccargia
➕ 167 D2 🕓 Apr–Oct daily 9–6:30 💶 €3

Sant' Antíoco di Bisarcio
➕ 167 E3 🕓 May–Sep Tue–Sun 9:30–1, 3–7; Oct–April Tue–Sun 10–1, 4–7 💶 €2

San Pietro di Sórres
➕ 167 E1 ℹ www.sanpietrodisorres.net
🕓 Mon–Sat 8–11, 2–4, 5–6

43 Valle dei Nuraghi & Nuraghe Santu Antine

Torralba is at the head of the Valle dei Nuraghi (Valley of the Nuraghi), 30km (19mi) south of Sássari. The valley is strewn with ancient complexes, but the biggest is the **Nuraghe Santu Antine** (▶ 118). The central dry-stone tower, made of basalt blocks, measures 17m (56ft). It was perhaps up to 21m (69ft) higher when it was built in around 1500BC, but it was partially

Dark Walls of Power

Santu Antine (▶ 117) is one of the largest Nuraghe complexes in Sardinia. Its walls and high central tower create an intriguing eye catcher on their highland plateau and make a clear claim to power that is underlined by the beauty and sheer size of the complex. Originally, the black edifice contrasted with the white limestone surrounding it: The Sards call the edifice "House of the King" (Sa Dómu de su Réi).

❶ Central Tower

It must once have been 22m (72ft) high. Beneath it is a large domed room, surrounded by a ring corridor. Steps set into the walls lead up to the first floor, which was apparently used as a gathering place for the "Council of Elders"; the stone ledge around the edge served as a place to sit. From the middle of the room, there is a view through the window to Nuraghe Oes, 800m away. The steps continue up to the second floor at a height of 17m (56ft); however the corbelled dome no longer exists.

❷ Corner Towers

The fortress was extended by adding three corner towers that were connected with Cyclopean walls. They towered above the platform of the triangular bastion.

❸ Inner Courtyard

The main entrance as well as the entrances to both corner towers and the central tower lead into the spacious, around 100m² (1,000ft²) inner courtyard with a fountain. The square was the armoury and coordination point, with connections to all parts of the Nuraghe castle.

❹ Defensive Walls

The double-storey defensive walls that lead to the rear tower and made it possible for soldiers to move quickly through the bastion are very impressive. Slits permit light to enter the wall-walks and were perhaps also used as embrasures (for shooting arrows).

The imposing Nuraghe Santu Antine is also called "House of the King"

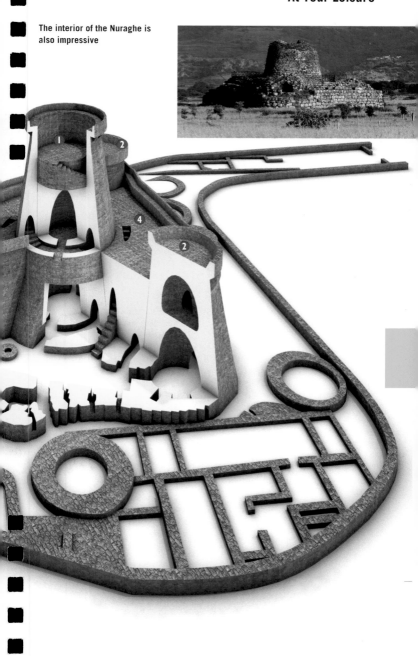

The interior of the Nuraghe is also impressive

demolished in the 19th century to build the village well in Torralba. Three later, smaller towers surround the compound, linked by trenches and corridors. A spiral ramp leads to the central tower's higher rooms. The Romans converted them into a fortress and they were transformed into a palace, known as "Sa Domo de Su Rei", by the early Christians.

Signposted from Santu Antine, **Sant'Andrea Priu** near Bonorva is a complex of tombs carved into a rock cliff, dating to between 4000BC and 3000BC. Used into medieval times as chapels. The "Tomba del Capo", the native's tomb – the largest on Sardinia is particularly impressive.

 Insider Tip

Nuraghe Santu Antine
✉ About 4km (2.5mi) south of Torralba
ℹ www.nuraghesantuantine.it
🕐 April–Sep 9–8; Oct–March 10–5 💶 €6

Sant'Andrea Priu
🕐 March–Oct 9:30–1, 3–dusk 💶 €3.50

44 Bosa

The SP105 from Alghero to Bosa is a gloriously undulating stretch of 42km (26mi) of coastal road before arriving at Bosa. A colony of about 100 griffon vultures nest in 🔭 **cliffs**

Insider Tip

at Capo Marargiu; a source of fascination for children and adults alike. The charming town of Bosa is clustered along the banks of the River Temo. Watching over the town is **Castello Malaspina**; its castle chapel, **Nostra Signora di Regnos Altos**, contains a wonderful 14th-century fresco cycle of famous saints. Stretching out beneath the castle, the medieval Old Town is well worth seeing.

A walk takes you along the Temo to the secluded church of **San Pietro extra muros** made of red trachyte. Built in 1073, the religious building numbers among the oldest Romanesque buildings on the island.

Situated at the mouth of the Temo is Bosa Marina which has a broad beach scattered with bars.
➕ 158 C7

Castello Malaspina
☎ 340 395 5048; www.castellodibosa.it
🕐 Daily March, Nov 10–1; April–June 10–7; July, Aug 10–7:30; Sep 10–6; Oct 10–5 💶 €4

San Pietro Extra Muros
🕐 April–June Tue–Sat 9:30–12:30, Sun 3:30–5:30; July, Aug Tue–Fri 9:30–12:30, Sat 9:30–12:30, 4–6, Sun 4–7; Sep, Oct Mon–Sat 9:30–12:30, Sun 3–5 💶 €2

Bosa: Old Town idyll at the foot of the Castello Malaspina

Where to...
Stay

Prices
Expect to pay per person for a meal, excluding drinks:
€ under €26   €€ €26–€55   €€€ over €55

SÁSSARI

Hotel Vittorio Emanuele €–€€
In the heart of the city, this pleasing former *palazzo* has been fully restored. The result is carefully furnished, comfortable rooms where style veers to modern minimalist, but not without murals. All the rooms have air conditioning and are soundproofed. There is a good restaurant, Platha de Cothinas, and a rustic stone cellar – perfect for wine-tasting.
🔒 166 C3
✉ Corso Vittorio Emanuele II 100/102
☎ 079 235 538; www.hotelvittorioemanuele.ss.it

ALGHERO

Hotel Angedras €€
Friendly, light three-star hotel with 31 Mediterranean-furnished rooms with a balcony. Five minutes to the sea and ten to the Old Town. *Insider Tip* Complimentary shuttle bus to the picturesque Maria Pia beach.
🔒 166 B2 ✉ Via Frank 2
☎ 079 973 5034; www.angedras.it

Hotel San Francesco €–€€
A former convent, this is Alghero's only hotel in the pretty Old Town. The best rooms overlook the cloisters of the Chiesa di San Francesco. The breakfast is taken in the cloisters.
🔒 166 B2 ✉ Via Ambrogio Machin 2
☎ 079 980 330; www.sanfrancescohotel.com

Hotel Villa Las Tronas €€€–€€€€
Spectacularly located on a private promontory overlooking the sea, this former Italian royal family holiday home is Alghero's most luxurious hotel. Antiques, marbled halls, chandeliers and rich brocades ooze opulence in this 19th-century castellated pleasure palace. There are two saltwater swimming pools, indoor and outdoor, a beauty centre, gym and a wellness centre.
🔒 166 B2 ✉ Lungomare Valencia 1
☎ 079 981 818;
www.hotelvillalastronas.it

BOSA

Corte Fiorita €–€€
In three different historic buildings, this collection of *alberghi* (inns) is in the heart of town. The rooms are rustic, light and spacious, with tiled floors, exposed stone walls and tasteful fabrics; a surplus is charged for a balcony or room with a view of the river. Breakfast can be taken in a walled courtyard at Le Palme, the check-in point for all properties.
🔒 170 C5 ✉ Lungo Temo De Gasperi 45
☎ 078 537 7058; www.albergo-diffuso.it

Hotel Palazzo Sa Pischedda €€
Art Nouveau palazzo directly by the Roman bridge on the Temo with frescoes by the painter Emilio Scherer and 15 rooms. The superior panorama rooms are particularly impressive with their large terrace and view over the Temo and Old Town. The Srestaurant dedicated to slow food is rightly praised.
🔒 170 C5 ✉ Via Roma 8
☎ 0785 373 065;
www.hotelsapischedda.com

Where to...
Eat and Drink

Prices
Expect to pay for a three-course set menu without drinks:

£ under £8   ££ £8–£12   £££ over £12

SÁSSARI

Caffè Florian ££
Elegantly mirrored and muralled, both Bar Caffè Florian and the more expensive next-door restaurant are good spots for dining. Tables spill onto the pavement from the bar's Toulouse-Lautrec-inspired interior, perfect for enjoying a *spremuta di arancia* (freshly squeezed blood orange juice) or cappuccino.

🞧 166 C3
✉ Bar Caffè Florian, Via Roma 6
✉ Florian, Via Capitano Bellieni 27
☎ 079 200 8056 🕐 Daily

Il Giamaranto ££–£££
Although the restaurant is rather unprepossessing on the outside, the menu inside is very appealing. Popular with the locals, Giamaranto is regarded as one of the best restaurants in town and serves traditional Sardinian and Italian dishes without the frills.

🞧 166 C3 ✉ Via Alghero 69
☎ 079 274 598; www.giamaranto.com
🕐 Closed Sat, Sun (summer) and Sun, Mon (winter)

Ristorante Giglio Al Mokádor £
This buzzing little place is popular with the locals and a good choice for inexpensive snacks and drinks. On Fridays there is happy hour 7–9pm, with *antipasti all'italiana*.

Insider Tip

🞧 158 C4 ✉ Largo Cavallotti 2, off Piazza Castello, near Via Roma
☎ 079 235 736
🕐 Daily lunch and dinner

Ristorante Liberty ££
Set in a small piazza in the town centre, next to the Corso Vittorio Emanuele, this elegantly restored restaurant was a small Liberty-style palazzo. The speciality is fish. The atmospheric wine/piano bar, with a stream running down the stone steps into the tasting cellar, serves a good selection of snacks.

🞧 166 C3 ✉ Piazza N Sauro 3
☎ 079 236 361
🕐 Tue–Sun, by reservation

ALGHERO

Trattoria Marco Polo ££
This small, family-run trattoria has a wide selection of very good dishes. The prices are extremely reasonable for the quality served. It is a pleasant location with just one down point: there is no al fresco dining.

🞧 166 B2 ✉ Via Cavour 46
☎ 079 973 8 76; www.trattoriamarcopolo.com
🕐 Daily dinner (from 6)

Buena Vista Bar €–€€
Actually, this restaurant should be called the "Sunset Club", because everyone meets here for a sundowner. The bar has a superb location on the town wall with a panoramic view of the Capo Cácchia. Unfortunately, on the narrow town wall space for tables is very limited and there is a great demand for the few there are. Cocktails cost about €6–€9.

🞧 166 B2
✉ Bastioni Marco Polo 47
🕐 Daily 3:30pm–3am

Focacceria Milese €

The food served at this simple eatery, *tavola calda,* is always fresh and not expensive. Its top sellers are *focacce,* available in many different varieties. They are by far the best and most reasonably priced in Alghero. The Focacceria is also very popular with the Algheresi, which is why the chairs overlooking the harbour promenade are nearly always occupied.

➕ 166 B2 ✉ Via Garibaldi 11
☎ 079 252 419; www.barmilese.it
🕐 Wed–Mon 7am–1am; closed Jan

Trattoria Al Refettorio €€

Chic, atmospheric wine bar with good nibbles. The restaurant food is also good – and there is outdoor, covered seating. Fish and seafood as well as dishes such as wild boar. As you would expect, it has a very good, extensive wine list.

➕ 166 B2 ✉ Carrerò del Porxo
(Vicolo Adami) 47, off Via Roma
☎ 079 973 1126; www.alrefettorio.it
🕐 Wed–Mon lunch and dinner;
daily in High season

Trattoria Caragol €€

Slightly off the beaten path, this trattoria has a cosy dining area. The friendly proprietor is happy to help you make your choice and tell you about his fresh regional dishes. You should try the macaroni and the *manjar blanc dessert.*

➕ 166 B2 ✉ Via Maiorca 73
☎ 079 973 8022

Trattoria Maristella €€

Small authentic trattoria on the edge of the Old Town near the Piazza Sulis, in which locals and tourist alike feel very much at home. The dishes are fresh and tasty, the prices fair and, as a result, the demand significant. When the restaurant opens at 7pm, it takes no time at all for it to fill up, so you need to reserve a table!

➕ 166 B2 BVia F. Kennedy 9 ☎ 079 97 8172
🕐 Tue–Sun lunch and dinner; closed Nov

STINTINO

Ristorante da Antonio €€

This welcoming family-run restaurant specializes in fish and seafood. Note that portions tend to be very generous and service is also very attentive, although the €3 *coperto* is way too expensive.

➕ 166 B4 ✉ Via Marco Polo 14
☎ 079 523 077 🕐 Daily lunch and dinner

BOSA

Borgo Sant'Ignazio €€

Follow the signs through the tangle of alleys of the Old Town up to this atmospheric bistro, with some tables outside. Specialities include local *aragosta* (lobster) as well as traditional Sardinian meat dishes. As it is on the Strada della Malvasia di Bosa (vineyards), it also has a good selection of Malvasia dessert wines to accompany typical Sardinian sweetmeats.

➕ 170 C5 ✉ Via Sant'Ignazio 33
☎ 0785 374 129; www.ristorantebosa.it
🕐 Tue–Sun 1–3, 7:30–11

Sa Pischedda €€

This excellent restaurant is part of the Slow Food movement. Prepare to linger over seasonal delicacies and Sardinian specialities. Also run by the hotel is the Ponte Vecchio, on a jetty above the river, which specializes in seafood.

➕ 170 C5 ✉ Via Roma 8
☎ 0785 373 065; www.hotelsapischedda.it
🕐 Closed Jan

CASTELSARDO

Baga Baga €€–€€€

This excellent hotel-restaurant scores high marks with its excellent panorama terrace, its dream view of the coast and the sea as well as its much acclaimed cuisine.

Insider Tip

➕ 167 D4 BLocalità La Terra Bianca
☎ 079 470 075; www.hotelbagabaga.it
🕐 April–Oct daily lunch and dinner;
closed Tue Dec–March and Nov

Where to...
Shop

In **Alghero** shop for clothes, shoes and leather goods, locally crafted ceramics, pottery, cork and hand-woven baskets, but refrain from buying any red coral to protect the coral banks in the Far East (because that is where it comes from!). Enjoy a nice stroll through the **indoor markets** on Via Sássari and Via Cagliari or the **weekly market** in Via Amalfi by the station (Mon–Sat 7–1).

At **Sella & Mosca Vineyards**, 10km (6mi) north of Alghero, you can taste and buy their celebrated wine – primarily fine whites, such as the Terre Biance or the Monteoro (► 111; www.sellaemosca.com).

In **Bosa**, apart from the fine embroidery (*Fileti di Bosa*), sold from windows or doors by the embroiderers, the famous Malvasia di Bosa should be at the top of the shopping list. The best is available from the **Columbu family** (www.malvasiacolumbu.com) in Via Marconi 1.

Everything the heart desires is on sale in **Sássari**. In the Old Town, you can find shops, workshops and boutiques, hypermarkets in the main shopping boulevards of Via Roma and Corso Vittorio Emanuele, and an **antique and flea market** in Via Santa Caterina (last Sun in the month 9–7).

One of the oldest businesses on Corso Vittorio Emanuele is the nostalgic **Bagella** (www.bagella.it), which has been selling everything in the way of Sard outfits from boots, jackets and belts to gold and silver jewellery since 1932.

In the wickerwork centre of **Castelsardo,** interest naturally focuses on the diverse selection of basket wares. The best places to buy it are either directly from the basket-makers in the Old Town or at the **ISOLA-Cooperativa Cestinale** (Via Roma 104).

Where to...
Go Out

You can jive to the beat of live jazz, Blues, rock and Ethno at **Pocoloco** (Via Gramsci 8, www.pocoloco alghero.com) all year round.

Another good address is also the **Ruscello** on the outskirts of the town towards Olmedo with three dance floors and a lounge with a garden (Loc. Angeli Custodi 57).

Disco-Club **El Tró** (Lungomare Valencia 3), directly by the sea, has been a hotspot in Alghero's nightlife since 1976.

The **Sássari** metropolis has an extremely diverse and high-quality cultural scene and, as a university city, a colourful club and pub scene.

Theatre buffs will enjoy the traditional **Teatro Civico** (Corso Vittorio Emanuele), the new **Nuovo Teatro** Comunale (Piazzale Cappuccini) or **Teatro di Tradizione** (Viale Umberto 72), while younger theatre enthusiasts should try the youth theatre Teatro Ferroviario.

Night owls meet from midnight in the **Triciclo Club** (Via Don Minzoni 20) to dance until 6, in the **Omega** (Via Carlo Felice 33) or at **Sgt. Pepper** (Via Asproni 20).

Among the town's many good pubs and cafés are **Accademia** (Via Torre Tonda 11), **Majoli Bar** (Emiciclo Garibaldi 5), **Tropicana Café** (Via Porcellana 3), **Dream Bar** (Via Cavour 15) and **Kristall-Bar** (Via Fancello 6).

The Northeast

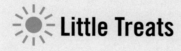 **Little Treats**

Off to Moon Valley

A path leads from Capo Testa to the legendary **Valle della Luna**, where a fabulous beach dotted with bizarre rock formations awaits you (➤ 138).

See Gallura from its prettiest side

In the heart of wonderful Gallura, the little **San Trano church** perched on a mountain not far from Luogosanto (➤ 137) conjures up an oasis of calm.

Feast in Palau

Top cuisine with a view of the Maddalena archipelago: **La Gritta** in Palau is a perfect choice (➤ 142).

Getting Your Bearings

Granite landscapes, fantastic formations of wind- and sea-sculpted rock, prehistoric stone dwellings and a beautiful, more discrete coastline scattered with islands and indented with picturesque coves – this is Gallura. The sea around here really does sparkle like a jewel and the Costa Smeralda – "Emerald Coast" – is outdazzled only by the bejewelled and glamorous people who flock to this exclusive playground.

Planes, boats, trains and buses arrive at Ólbia, a convenient gateway to the pleasures of this beautiful region. The booming town has developed a lively centre with shops and businesses, cafés and bars, and it is nice just to stroll through the streets and take it all in.

The fabled Costa Smeralda is within easy reach of Ólbia, and the Pevero coastline has glorious white sandy beaches and turquoise seas. Near by are resorts such as Cannigione and Santa Teresa di Gallura, which are less glitzy but still bask along beautiful stretches of coast.

Palau is the gateway to the seven islands of the Arcipélago de La Maddalena, where a highlight is La Caprera, the home and resting place of Giuseppe Garibaldi.

The interior of the Gallura seems worlds apart from the pleasures of the beach. Arzachena is a true Sardinian town and worth visiting for its excellent prehistoric sites. The old capital of Gallura, Témpio Pausánia, is an hour's drive away through beautiful countryside at the foot of the Monte-Limbara mountain. In this region of great contrasts, it is a delight to discover yet another side of Sardinia.

The "Bear of Palau" on the Costa Smeralda

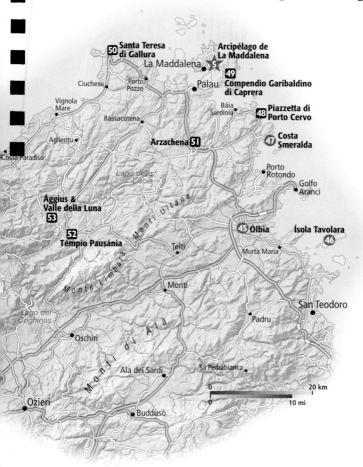

Four Perfect Days

If you're not quite sure where to begin your travels, this itinerary recommends a practical and enjoyable four days exploring the northeast of Sardinia, taking in some of the best places to see. For more information see the main entries (➤ 130–138).

Day 1

Morning
In 45 **Ólbia** (right; ➤ 132), walk up to the old part of town and the Corso Umberto. Take time to visit the Basilica di San Simplicio and the Archaeological Museum at the Old Harbour. After a coffee break on the Piazza Margherita, make your way to Porto San Paólo to take a boat trip to 46 **Ísola Tavolara** (➤ 133).

Lunch
Eat at **Ristorante da Tonino** (➤ 141) on Ísola Tavolara, then spend the afternoon relaxing on the beach.

Afternoon
Back in Óbia, take the wonderful coastal road to Golfo Aranci and enjoy the lovely view of the coast and their picture book beaches. An ideal place for a meal in a relaxing atmosphere is **Manzoni** by the fishing harbour. Stylish accommodation awaits you at **Locanda del Conte Mameli** (➤ 139) in Ólbia.

Day 2

Arcipélago de La Maddalena
50 Santa Teresa di Gallura
5 49 Compendio Garibaldino di Caprera
Piazzetta di Porto Cervo 48
Arzachena 51
47 Costa Smeralda
Ággius & Valle della Luna 53
52
Témpio Pausánia
Ólbia 45
46 Ísola Tavolara

Morning
Set off for the legendary 47 **Costa Smeralda** (➤ 134) Drive via Cala di Volpe to Porto Rotondo and to Porto Cervo. Fashion fans can admire the shop windows of Armani & Co around the central 48 **Piazetta di Porto Cervo** (➤ 136) and drink what may turn out to be the most expensive Cappuccino they have ever had.

Lunch
At lunchtime leave Porto Cervo and drive up to the nearby little mountain village San Pantaleo to **Ristorante Da Nico** (➤ 142).

Afternoon
Take a boat trip or relax on the beaches. **Hotel S'Olias** (➤ 140) is a good address for both food and accommodation.

Day 3

Morning
Set off to visit the ☆**Arcipélago de La Maddalena** (➤ 130). There are regular ferries from Palau, which you can take as a foot passenger or with a car. Enjoy a stroll around the old town of La Maddalena and have a coffee in the Piazza Garibaldi. Alternatively, you can also do a day trip by boat to the island world of the Maddalena archipelago with refreshing swimming breaks and lunch.

Afternoon
Enjoy exploring the island of Caprera (accessible also by road), perhaps with a visit to **49 Compendio Garibaldino di Caprera** (➤ 136), Garibaldi's home and museum. Return to the Palau and enjoy a lovely evening on the terrace of the **Ristorante La Gritta** (➤ 142).

Day 4

Morning
Set off for the little mountain town of **51 Arzachena** (➤ 137), ideally on Wednesdays, when there is a market. Il Fungo, an enormous mushroom-shaped cliff dominates the landscape here. There are important archaeological sites in the surrounding area, such as Albucciu, Malchittu, the Giants' tomb Coddu Vecchiu (picture below) and Li Lolghi.

Lunch
It would be hard to find a more beautiful place for lunch than this enchanting **Jaddhu** (➤ 141) not far from Coddu Vecchiu.

Afternoon
Though cork oak woods, the journey continues up towards the little mountain town of **52 Tempio Pausánia**, characterised by its mainly granite buildings and plentiful springs (➤ 138). After taking a stroll through the Old Town, you must go and see **53 Ággius** (➤ 138), which is famous for its traditional weaving crafts. Two very attractive museums are also located here: Museo Etnografico and Museo del Banditismo.

⑤Arcipélago de La Maddalena

Seven dreamy islands with Caribbean-blue seas make up the archipelago north of the Costa Smeralda. The only developed island is La Maddalena itself, from where there is a causeway to Garibaldi's island, La Caprera. But there are boat trips to see the other islands, including Spargi and Budelli with its glorious pale pink beach, Spiaggia Rosa.

Rocks hewn over thousands of years characterize the landscape of the Gallura, and on La Maddalena there are about 150 of these *tafoni* whose shapes have earned them nicknames such as Rabbit Rock, De Gaulle, Dinosaur, Eagle's Beak, and even Il Mostro di Lochness (Loch Ness Monster).

La Maddalena Town
The most popular way of getting to La Maddalena is by the 20-minute ferry crossing from Palau to La Maddalena town. This is a bustling place with cobbled streets and piazzas, and a decorous *passeggiata* along the Via Garibaldi, the main street connecting Piazza Umberto I to Piazza Garibaldi. There are also some good restaurants around the squares and pleasant bars in which to people-watch.

There are few sights, but the **Museo Diocesano** has some fascinating exhibits, including gifts from Lord Horatio Nelson. The Commander of the British fleet made regular visits here aboard *Victory* from 1803 to 1805 to keep an eye on the French fleet anchored in the port of Toulon. He struck up a good relationship with Agostino Millelire, Commander of the Port of La Maddalena, and on his departure, presented two silver candlesticks and a crucifix to the church, **Chiesa di Santa Maria Maddalena**. Proudly displayed in the museum with the silver "treasures" is Nelson's letter of 18 October 1804 thanking the inhabitants for their treatment of his fleet. There is also a huge display of *ex voto* gifts, including 500 rings.

INSIDER INFO

Insider Tip

- Those lucky enough, to be **on holiday with their own boat**, can anchor off the Ísola di Santa Maria and go ashore to **La Casitta** (tel: 329 370 5621, www.lacasitta.com; May–Oct), once the home of a shepherd, now an exclusive restaurant in a prime setting, where guests can enjoy a gourmet candlelit meals while they look out over the ocean.
- It is understandable why people refer to Cala Coticcio on La Caprera as **Cala Tahiti**. Overland, it is an arduous one-hour walk across impressive rocky landscape to reach this paradisiacal part of the world.

Evening atmosphere in La-Maddalena town

Out of the centre on the road to Cala Spalmatore (about 1km/0.6mi) you come to the **Museo Archeológico Navale** on Via Panoramica. The main exhibits are of a Roman cargo ship that was wrecked in the waters of the archipelago around 120BC, showing a reconstructed cross-section of the hull and amphorae.

La Caprera

To the east of the island a causeway links to pine-covered La Caprera. As well as visiting the Garibaldi museum (➤ 136), this is a pleasant place to walk or cycle around (➤ 155).

Beaches

The best beaches on La Maddalena are Cala Maiore, Spiaggia Spalmatore, Cala Lunga and Spiaggia Monte di Rena. On Caprera there are Cala Napoletana and Cala Serena in the west and, in the east, Cala Brigantino and Cala Coticcio.

TAKING A BREAK

A wonderful oasis in Caprera's nature reserve is **I Mille**. The kiosk sells excellent *panini*, *salsiccias* and other snacks, which can be eaten at the table and in hammocks under the pines; the cheerful twittering of the birds is a complimentary extra.

Insider Tip

➕ 169 D5
🚢 Regular ferries from Palau. During the day at 15-minute intervals, and at night every hour. Journey time every 15 minutes.

Museo Diocesano
✉ Chiesa di S Maria Maddalena, Via Baron Manno ☎ 0789 737 400
🕐 Tue–Sun 10–1, 3–7 and 9:30–11:30 June–Sep 🎟 €2

Museo Archeológico Navale
✉ Via Panoramica ☎ 0789 790 660
🕐 Mon–Sat 10–1 🎟 €2

㊺ Ólbia

Ólbia, which is the Greek word for "happy" or "rich", was founded by the Punics and prospered as an important Roman harbour and trading centre. With its harbour and airport, Sardinia's flourishing boom town has once again become the most important traffic hub on the island.

On arrival at Ólbia, which is one of the island's main entry points, you could be forgiven for trying to get out of it as quickly as possible. However, the cobbled lanes in the old part of town around **Corso Umberto** are full of good restaurants and pretty piazzas. From here, past the railway station, you come to the town's top sight, the **Basilica di San Simplicio**. This 11th to 12th century Pisan Romanesque church is hewn out of Galluran granite. Inside there are columns and other pieces of masonry salvaged from Phoenician and Roman temples. In the apse there are two 13th-century frescoes, the left-hand one of which depicts San Simplicio, the patron saint of Ólbia. His feast day on 15 May brings the city's biggest celebration, lasting for three days and centred around the old church. Fortunately for those who don't want to linger here, Ólbia has good bus connections from the airport and the ferry terminal and, from the city centre, to Cagliari and other cities by train and to all parts of the region bus.

A café in Piazza Margherita, Ólbia

TAKING A BREAK

Enjoy the street life at one of the many **outdoor cafés** or restaurants along Corso Umberto and the central Piazza Margherita.

✚ 169 D2/3

46 Ísola Tavolara

Just 1km (0.6mi) wide and 4km (2.5mi) long, but more than 564m (1,850ft) high, the huge Tavolara rock rises out of the sea like some sort of prehistoric sea monster. Located in the centre of a marine protected area and the habitat of many different species, Tavolara is one of the landmarks of Sardinia and, believe it or not, also a kingdom.

The mighty Tavolara rock

The eastern side of Tavolara is a military zone, but there's free access to the inhabited western side, which even has a cemetery. Here are the **tombs of Tavolara's kings**.

When King Carlo Alberto of Sardinia visited the island in 1833 for a spot of goat hunting and feasting, he thanked its only inhabitant, the Corsican fisherman Giuseppe Bertoleoni, by "crowning" him an independent sovereign monarch. Since then the island's "kings" have all descended from the Bertoleoni family; the present sovereign, Carlo II, runs Ristorante da Tonino (➤ 141). Wild goats still roam and it is a paradise for birds. On the southern tip there's a good beach at **Spalmatore di Terra**.

Tavolara island hosts an **open-air film festival** at which numerous actors from the participating films as well as famous actors mingle with the audience. For more information visit www.cinematavolara.it.

Boat rides to the Tavolara and neighbouring Isola Molara are easy to find in the little beach town of Porto San Paolo. Lining the coast, south of Porto San Paolo, you will find one bathing paradise after another, some large, some small, but all displaying Caribbean beauty. The sandy beaches of Porto Istana bay are of picture-postcard calibre, the famous La Cinta beach near San Teodoro legendary, the beaches at Puntalida and Lu Impostu magnificent, the enchanting Cala Brandinchi on the Capo Coda Cavallo unique, and the beach along the Cala di Budoni miles and miles long.

Insider Tip

✚ 169 E2

④⑦ Costa Smeralda

The waters of the Emerald Coast sparkle like a precious jewel, reflected in the diamonds of those who flock to this millionaires' playground. In the 1950s the Aga Khan fell in love with the sandy beaches and idyllic coves along this coastal strip and made it an exclusive resort. But the charms of this coastline are not confined to the "Smeralda"; gorgeous beaches and bays are all around.

The Costa Smeralda begins around 12km (7.5mi) north of Ólbia and extends just 10km (6mi) between the Golfo di Cugnana and Golfo di Arzachena, but has a beautiful 56km (35-mile) coastline. The area has stuck firmly by the guiding principle that all development should blend into the **superb scenery** without disfiguring it in any way. So there are no high-rise buildings; telephone wires and electrical cables have to be hidden underground; and the buildings are a curious mix of Aegean island, contemporary and Moroccan styles.

Porto Cervo
Porto Cervo is the only real town and "capital" of the area. Imitating a Mediterranean fishing village, it's a pleasant place to stroll, to see and be seen – and to window shop (► 136). It all tends to be very quiet during the day as everyone is relaxing on their boat, in a villa or on the beach.

Other Resorts
The Pevero coastline that has made Sardinia so famous is lined with beaches and coves accessed by fabulous villas and luxury hotels – e.g. the Romazzino, the Pitrizza and the hotel that became famous for its role in the James Bond film *The Spy Who Loved Me*: Cala di Volpe.
　　On the eastern side of the Golfo di Cugnana is **Porto Rotondo**. It is a chic resort with obligatory marina, and is the site of Silvio Berlusconi's €400 million Villa La Certosa. Not really part of the Costa Smeralda, as it was developed

View out over the harbour bay of Porto Cervo

later, this coast also has beautiful beaches. To the south, the resort of **Golfo Aranci** lies on the tip of Capo Figari. This is more of a family resort, with lovely beaches helpfully numbered from one to five – the third of which, "La Terza Spiaggia", is the best.

Also within easy reach of Costa Smeralda is **Cannigione** on the Gulf of Arzachena – an attractive, lively village with a picturesque port and marina. You can still sport your Prada shades but you're not so likely to go over your credit limit here. The nearby headland, **Capo d'Orso**, is a huge, bear-shaped rock. It is 122m (400ft) high and affords stunning views.

With their crystal-clear waters, the dream beaches of the Costa Smeralda are reminiscent of the Caribbean

TAKING A BREAK

The family-friendly **Da Nico** (➤ 142) in San Pantaleo in the hinterland of Costa Smeralda is a village pizzeria in the best sense. Everything is good here, from the huge and delicious pizzas to the pasta, fish and meat dishes.

➕ 169 E4

INSIDER INFO

- Anyone who comes to Palau must go and visit the **Capo d'Orso** which soars up to the east of the town. A very pretty and easy trail leads from the car park up to the gigantic weathered rock in the form of a bear (parking fee: €2; admission: €2). At the top, you are rewarded with a spectacular view of Palau and the strait between Sardinia and Corsica including the Maddalena archipelago. *Insider Tip*

- The lovely beach **Portu Li Coggi** (or Spiaggia del Principe, the Prince's Beach), is poorly signposted, but is really worth a little effort. From Cala di Volpe, head south on SP160 for about 2km (1.2mi). Before Capriccioli take the junction for Romazzino on the left. Head north and near the resort (1.5km) take a right on Via Asfodeli towards the sea to a barrier preventing car access. From here a 600m track takes you to the shore. *Insider Tip*

At Your Leisure

48 Piazzetta di Porto Cervo

The Piazzetta is full of cool archways, loggias, bars and shops. Members of the international jet set rub shoulders with tourists and there are numerous designer boutiques to drool over. All the usual suspects are here, including Bulgari, Dolce & Gabbana and Valentino, where a pair of shoes will set you back €1,000 at a conservative estimate. Overlooking the Piazzetta is the Cervo Hotel, a gorgeous spot to indulge in a sundowner – although only if you are suitably dressed and have sufficient funds with you. Even a small Coca-Cola costs €15 here.

🚩 169 D4

49 Compendio Garibaldino di Caprera

Revered even in his own lifetime as the father of the Italian nation, Giuseppe Garibaldi (1807–82) made La Caprera his home in 1855. It was his refuge after his campaigns in the pursuit of unification, and he found solace in the peace.

In the courtyard stands a majestic pine planted by Garibaldi on the day his daughter Celia was born (he had seven children by three wives and one by a governess).

Compendio Garibaldino di Caprera

The house, Casa Bianca, has changed little since his death. His personal effects include his trademark red shirt *(camicia rossa)*, after which his troops – the Red Shirts – were named, and two embroidered fez hats. The rooms are small and simple, with the exception of his death chamber. Built at the request of his wife, Francesca, it looks out towards Nice, the city of his birth. In this room a calendar shows the date of his death, 2 June 1882. His tomb in the garden is made of rough granite. Visitors are not allowed to use mobile phones in the Garibaldi Museum!

🚩 169 D4 ✉ Compendio Garibaldino di Caprera
☎ 0789 727 162; www.compendiogaribaldino.it
🕐 June–Sep Tue–Sun 9–8
💷 €6; under 18s free of charge.

50 Santa Teresa di Gallura & Capo Testa

Lying on the northernmost tip of the island, this is now a very popular summer resort. From the main Piazza Vittorio Emanuele, the Via del Mare leads to the 16th-century Spanish watchtower,

Santa Teresa di Gallura

Roccia Il Fungo (Mushroom Rock) is on Via Limbara in Arzachena

Torre di Langosardo. From here you can drink in the glorious views over the Strait of Bonifacio to Corsica. A path leads west of the tower to the main beach, Spiaggia Rena Bianca. Ferries leave daily for the 20-minute trip across to Bonifacio on Corsica – a great day out for a French lunch and some shopping. There are also boat trips to the Maddalena islands.

The top sight here is the fantastic **Capo Testa**, which the Sards calls the "Cimitero di Sassi" (cemetery of stones). Wind and waves have transformed this granite cape into an enchanting rock garden with bizarre shapes. Just before you get to the car park, a trail leads off to the legendary Valle della Luna with its fantastic rock formations and enchanting beach – a lovely place for a 👪 picnic with the entire family.
➕ 168 B5

Torre di Longosardo
🕐 Nov–April Mon, Wed, Fri 3:30–4:30; May–Oct 10:30–1, 4–6 💶 €2

🗺 Arzachena
Giants' tombs and megalithic stone circles in the prehistoric remains dotted in the woods and fields around Arzachena, about half an hour's drive from Ólbia. The **Nuraghe Albucciu**, 2km (1mi) southeast of

the town, is one of Gallura's best-preserved nuraghi. It has an unusual granite roof that is flat rather than conical. A footpath leads from the car park near the Nuraghe to the 2km (1.2mi) distant Stone Age **Tempietto Malchittu**. About 4km (2.5mi) south of Arzachena is Coddu Vecchiu, one of the island's most complete "giants' tombs". The original corridor tomb is estimated to date to the 18th to 16th centuries BC, before it was extended in Nuraghic times by adding a forecourt edged by stone.

Close by are the Tomba dei Giganti di Li Lolghi and **Necropoli di Li Muri**. Li Lolghi rises on a hillock and, although similar to Coddu Vecchiu, is nearly twice as long in the inner chamber. The necropolis of Li Muri is reached by returning on the rough track to the left fork going west off the track from the road signposted Luogosanto. This burial site is estimated to date back to 3500BC and consists of several rectangular tombs of stone slabs encircled by smaller slabs. There are five central circles that contained bodies buried in a crouching position. Beside each tomb there are standing stones and small stone boxes. At the car park near the Nuraghe Albucciu you can get tickets, information and a map of

A craggy mountain in the lunar landscape known as Valle della Luna

the archaeological site. Admission fees range from €3 to €18 for all the sites. A new museum is the **Museo ETA Nuragica**, which is dedicated to showing everyday life of the Nuraghic civilization (ceramics, tools, clothes, food etc.).

➕ 168 C4

Nuraghe Albucciu/Templetto Malchittu
🕐 April–Oct daily 9 until an hour before sunset

Nuraghe La Prisgiona
🕐 March, April daily 10–6; May–Sep 10–8; Oct, Nov 10–7; Dec–Feb 10–4

Tomba Giganti Coddu Vecchiu
🕐 May–Sep 9–8; Oct–April 9–7

Tomba dei Giganti di Li Lolghi
🕐 May–Sep 10–1, 4–8; Oct–April 10–1, 3–7

Museo ETA Nuragica
✉ Località Tiana, on the SS125 towards Palau, Km 345
☎ 333 738 9973; www.anemosarzachena.com
🕐 15 May to 5 Sep Mon–Sat 10–1, 3:30–7:30; Mon, Wed, Fri, Sat 10–1, and Tue, Thu 5–8 rest of year 💶 €3

52 Témpio Pausánia

In the embrace of cork oak woods at the foot of Monte Limbara, North Sardinia's highest mountain range, is this charming little mountain village Témpio Pausánia. The cork centre of the island is a traditional summer resort, to which there is a light railway service from the coast (Palau) during the season!

Témpio Pausánia is an ideal starting point for hiking tours (info/maps available from Tourist Information). Those who do not want to walk up can actually drive almost to the summit.

➕ 168 B2

53 🍴 Ággius & Valle della Luna

Lying 10km (6mi) west of Témpio, the hill village **Ággius** is famous for its handicrafts, especially woven carpets (➤ 33), which are still made by hand and sold at an exhibition centre. The **Museo Etnográfico** gives a fascinating insight into this craft and traditions of inland Gallura. The **Museo del Banditismo** is also interesting. A scenic route around the village and through the mountains leads via the mountain valley to **Valle della Luna**. There is a great view from the car park on SP74 across to Ággius on the opposite side of the valley.

➕ 168 B3

Museo Etnográfico
✉ Via Monti di Lizu
☎ 079 621 029; www.museodiaggius.it
🕐 May to 15 Oct Tue–Sun 10–1, 3–7; 16 Oct to April 10–1, 3:30–5:30; closed Jan.
💶 €4

Museo del Banditismo
✉ Via Pretura ☎ 079 621 029
🕐 April to 15 Oct Tue–Sun 10–1, 4–6; 16 Oct to March Tue–Sun 10–1; closed Jan
💶 €4

Where to...
Stay

Prices
Expect to pay for a double room per night:
€ under €90   €€ €90–€155   €€€ €155–€250   €€€€ over €250

ÓLBIA

Hotel Cavour €–€€
This small hotel with 21 rooms is in the centre of Ólbia's old town. Tastefully refurbished, it is mostly cool white with pastel shades. There is a pleasant outdoor terrace, where breakfast is served in summer, and on-site parking.

➕ 169 D2/3
✉ Via Cavour 22
☎ 0789 204 033;
www.hotelcavourolbia.it

Hotel Centrale €€
The rooms of this, as its name indicates, very centrally located four-star hotel are relatively small, but tastefully furnished in a modern style and for the location and category very reasonable.

➕ 169 D2/3
✉ Corso Umberto 85
☎ 0789 23017;
www.hotelcentraleolbia.it

La Locanda del Conte Mameli €€–€€€
Feel like a member of the aristocracy in this meticulously restored and authentically furnished 18th-century Palazzo. The six rooms and two junior suites right in the heart of Ólbias exude nostalgic charm. Attached to the hotel is the neighbouring "Residenze del Conte" with eleven no less appealing rooms (1–3 rooms).

➕ 169 D2/3
✉ Via delle Terme 8
☎ 0789 23008;
www.lalocandadelcontemameli.com

COSTA SMERALDA

Cala di Volpe €€€€
The first luxury hotel of Costa Smeralda, Cala di Volpe is the glitziest of all the Starwood Hotels' Luxury Collection and at the same time the primordial mother of the neo-Sardinian style. Designed by French star architect Jacques Couelle to replicate a fishing village, **piccolo** *Paradiso* around its own little harbour, the hotel has welcomed many high-calibre guests from the international jet set, aristocracy as well as VIPs such as Carla Bruni, George Clooney and Liz Hurley. For around €30,000 per night, can stay in the 300m² (3,230ft²) President's Suite which has its own wine cellar. There are no rooms available for under €600 per night, but for that you can expect the best and finest of everything, for example a hung seawater pool or a golf course right on the coast.

➕ 169 D4
✉ Porto Cervo
☎ 0789 976 111; www.caladivolpe.com
🌞 May–Oct

Hotel Abi d'Oru €€€–€€€€
Lying on the Marinella Gulf, 6km (3.5mi) from Porto Rotondo, this salmon-coloured resort-style five-star hotel is located on a beautiful bay. Most of the 170 luxurious rooms enjoy sea views. In the grounds there is a large freshwater swimming pool, a lake that attracts birdlife and chanting

frogs, and paths leading down to the white sandy beach. There are two bars and two restaurants and a pizzeria on the beach. Facilities include a children's club and tennis courts.

➕ 169 D3
✉ Golfo di Marinella, Porto Rotondo
☎ 0789 309 019; www.hotelabidoru.it
🕑 Apr–Oct

Hotel Porto Piccolo €€–€€€

There is lovely view from here of the Gulf of Cugnana and the island lying before the coast of Caprera. This very peaceful four-star residence on a hill outside the town offers a selection of rooms and apartments. The spectacular and, in its own special way, unique Phi Beach Club is only a few minutes away.

Insider Tip

➕ 169 D3 ✉ Báia Sardínia ☎ 0789 99383; www.hotelportopiccolo.it 🕑 May to start of Oct

Hotel S'Olias €–€€

Very small and pretty family hotel in a secluded location with a view of the Golfo di Cugnano and the mountains near San Pantaleo. The picturesque complex in traditional Gallura "stazzu" style has ten spacious rooms that match the Sardinian architectural style and all have a panoramic terrace. A pool and the upmarket restaurant with its panorama terrace make the S'Olias that is reasonably priced for the region a very attractive choice.

➕ 169 C3 ✉ Loc. Ancioggiu,
(on SP13 from Arzachena to Cannigione)
☎ 0789 88598; www.solias.it
🕑 All year

SANTA TERESA DI GALLURA

Marinaro €–€€

This pleasant peach-coloured three-star hotel is in the centre of the town in a quiet street, but close to the beach. Inside, green and white stripes are the signature colours, and the airy bedrooms have been tastefully refurbished.

Rooms have balconies and there are lovely views from the top floor. There is also a good restaurant. It is family run with charming, helpful staff.

➕ 168 B5
✉ Via Angioy 48
☎ 0789 754 112;
www.hotelmarinaro.it

ARZACHENA

Tenuta Pilastru €–€€

An oasis of calm for those who wish to get away from the stress of their everyday life. Located about 5km (3mi) away from Arzachena, totally secluded in Gallura's wonderfully unspoilt and rugged landscape with its numerous "tafoni" rocks, this rural resort pleases its guests with its pool, spa centre and fantastic food. Clustered around the central building are beautiful little stone bungalows with a total of 32 charming rooms, all with a terrace. A perfect place from which to set off and explore the Maddalena islands and their beaches – or just enjoy the peace and quiet from the terrace.

Insider Tip

➕ 168 C4 ✉ Località Pilastru
(on the road to Bassacutena)
☎ 0789 82936; www.tenutapilastru.it

ÁGGIUS

Residence de Charme La Vignaredda €–€€

Charming accommodation in a peaceful location near the museum. All of the rooms and apartments are tastefully and stylishly furniture. The rooms with a balcony and a view of the well-kept garden are particularly nice. The apartments have a small kitchen. The great breakfast is very recommendable (not included in the price of the room) and includes many home-made products. Cristina and Maria Teresa are the good souls of the house.

➕ 168 B3 BVia Gallura 14
☎ 079 620 818; www.lavignaredda.it
🕑 All year

Where to...
Eat and Drink

Prices
Expect to pay per person for a meal, excluding drinks:
€ under €26   €€ €26–€55   €€€ over €55

ÓLBIA

Da Antonio €
Delicious food at reasonable prices is served in this trattoria in the centre of Ólbia.
➕ 169 D2/3 ✉ Via Garibaldi 48
☎ 0789 609 082

Il Mattacchione €–€€
Small, appealing trattoria with a short but select menu of five-star dishes at fair prices, which is why it is also very popular with the Sardinians as well. Awaiting you at this restaurant on Ólbia's largest shopping boulevard, just outside the main centre, are the talented chefs Giuseppe and Rosella, who speak perfect English.
➕ 169 D2/3 ✉ Viale Aldo Moro 351
☎ 380 240 5368 ⏰ Daily lunch and dinner

ÍSOLA TAVOLARA

Ristorante da Tonino €€
Tonino's is run by the present-day "king" of Tavolara (his coat of arms decorates the restaurant). There is an enticing veranda on the beach and the speciality is fish and seafood, served with great aplomb. Bar service includes sandwiches and snacks.
➕ 169 E3 ✉ Ísola Tavolara 14
☎ 078 958 570; www. ristorantereditavolara.com
⏰ Lunch and dinner; closed Tue

COSTA SMERALDA

Mezzaluna €€
In this family-run "half-moon" restaurant, in a pleasantly relaxed atmosphere, guests can enjoy seafood dishes awarded a distinction by the Federazione Italiana Cuochi or a simple pizza. The prices are reasonable, the service friendly and professional.
➕ 169 D3 ✉ Báia Sardínia, Località La Crucitta ☎ 0789 99311; www.ristorantemezzalunabajasardinia.com
⏰ Daily lunch and dinner

Antonella & Gigi €€
This rustic, family-run restaurant is very good value for the location, serving simply prepared classics such as *insalata di mare* (seafood salad), *prosciutto e melone* (melon and ham) and grilled fish.
➕ 169 D3
✉ Villa Punta Nuraghe 1, Porto Rotondo
☎ 0789 34238 ⏰ Wed–Mon noon–3, 7–11

Mama Latina €€
This restaurant that is located slightly inland is as popular with locals as it is with visitors. It is open all year round and pleasantly inexpensive.
➕ 169 D3 ✉ Loc. Cala di Volpe
☎ 0789 96026; www.mamalatina.it
⏰ April–Sep daily; Oct–March Mon–Sat

Jaddhu €€
Close to the Giants' Grave Coddu Vecchiu and the Nuraghe Prisgiona, this dream location right out in the middle of the countryside serves excellent food and has enchanting rooms. An ideal place to relax over a good meal.
➕ 168 C3 ✉ Arzachena, Loc. Capichera
☎ 0789 80636; www.jaddhu.com
⏰ Mid-May to mid-Oct daily, lunch and dinner

ARZACHENA

Da Nico €–€€

Although the setting is quite simple, the food is really delicious and reasonably price. Regardless of whether you order pizza, pasta, fish or meat, everything is good and fresh. The chef and his team are very friendly.

☐ 168 D3

✉ Via Zara 18, San Pantaleo ☎ 0789 65476; www.ristorantisanpantaleodanico.it

PALAU

La Gritta €€

The meals served at this restaurant that has been run by the Pierro family for 30 years are just as exceptional as the spectacular view of the sea and the Maddalena archipelago. To be able to enjoy the sunset on the terrace followed by the delights on the menu is a cultural and culinary highlight. During the season, you have to order a table in advance!

Insider Tip

☐ 168 C4 ✉ Loc. Porto Farao, Palau
☎ 0789 708 045; www.ristorantelagritta.it
🕙 15 April to 15 Sep daily; closed Wed rest of year

Where to...
Shop

The commercial centre of the region is **Ólbia**. There are many small shops in the Old Town and various stores on the central Piazza Margherita. The main shopping boulevard, however, is the long Via Roma outside the historical centre, which is also the address of the ceramics manufacturer, **Cera Sarda** (www.cerasarda.it). The largest shopping centre (**Auchan**) is located on the SS125 going towards San Teodoro.

One of the best white wines in Sardinia can be found at the **Azienda Capichera** (www.capichera. it) near Arazachena. or in Tempio Pausania in **Cantina Gallura** (www. cantinagallura.it). One of the most unusual boutiques on the island is the cork designer **Anna Grindi** in Tempio Pausania, Via Roma 34.

Tappete Aggese, traditional woven products, are available from **Laboratorio Tessile Artigianale Prof. Cannas** in Ággius (Via Li Criasgi 22).

A nice option is to buy home-produced cheese, ham and other specialities from the colourful **weekly markets** (Mon in Cannigione, Wed in Arzachena, Fri in Palau and Sat in Tempio).

Where to...
Go Out

The beating heart of Sardinia's nightlife is Costa Smeralda, and in the summer the clubs are the meeting places of the rich and famous. Anyone who wants to party there needs to be young, female and beautiful or in possession of a gold credit card. Those who manage to get past the doorman can dance with Paris Hilton and Co.

The jeunesse dorée meets in Flavio Briatores Club **Billionaire** (www.billionairelife.com), in the top discos **Ritual** (www.ritual.it) and **Heaven** (www.heavenportorotondo. com) or in the unique **Phi Beach Club** (www.phibeach.com). Less demanding in terms of dress code, and at €30 admission downright cheap in comparison are the discos opposite **Sopravento** (myspace. com/sopraventoclub) and **Sottovento** (myspace.com/sottoventoclub). There is no admission fee to **Mama Beach** (www.mamabeach.com) at Pittulongu, Ólbia.

Walks & Tours

1 CAGLIARI
Walk

DISTANCE 4km (2.5mi)   **TIME** 3–4 hours
START POINT Bastione San Remy ✚ 178 C2
END POINT Via Roma ✚ 178 C3

View over Cagliari's Old Town

This walk takes you from the heart of medieval Cagliari at the Bastione San Remy, past the amphitheatre and botanic garden, down to the café-lined Via Roma.

1–2

Start your walk from atop **Bastione San Remy** (➤ 48) on Piazza Costituzione. Heading north from the Bastione, walk up the Via Fossario to Piazza Palazzo, the heart of the Castello district, and you will see the **Cattedrale** (➤ 50) on your right. Look at the Pisan Romanesque-style facade and then go inside to see the baroque/Gothic decorations. The next building on your left, on the north-eastern side of the Piazza Palazzo, is the **Palazzo Viceregio**, its pale

green neoclassical facade contrasting with the deep rust shutters (Tue–Fri 9–1, Sat 9–2; free). The reception rooms are adorned with Murano glass chandeliers, frescoed ceilings and silk-lined walls – and portraits of the Piedmontese viceroys who formerly governed Sardinia from here.

2–3

Continue northwards and turn right into the little Piazzetta Mercede Mundula. From here there are glorious views over the bay and convenient benches from which to admire them. Continue up the Via Pietro Martini to the Piazza Indipendenza. At the head of this piazza is the **Torre di San Pancrazio** (Tue–Sun 9–5; entry fee €4). Similar to the Torre dell'Elefante (➤ 50), this is one of the city's medieval constructions not to have undergone "ruinous modification", as the plaque tells you. It was built by the Pisans in 1305 and is 55m (180ft) high; from the top there are spectacular views. Proceed through the archway to reach the sloping Piazza Arsenale and arrive at the **Cittadella dei Musei**.

3–4

There are four museums here – the Pinacoteca (art gallery); the Mostra di Cere Anatomiche, a waxworks of rather gory anatomic sections; the Museo d'Arte Siamese (Southeast Asian art); and the highlight, the **Museo Archeológico Nazionale** (➤ 51).

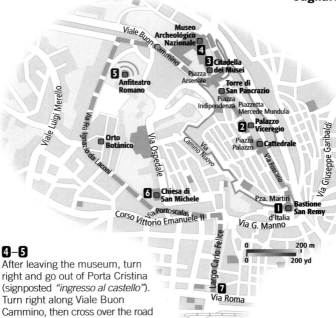

4–5

After leaving the museum, turn right and go out of Porta Cristina (signposted *"ingresso al castello"*). Turn right along Viale Buon Cammino, then cross over the road with Via Anfiteatro on your left and walk under the jacaranda trees to the **Anfiteatro Romano** on your left.

At the next junction, turn left down Via Frà Ignazio da Laconi to the entrance to the Anfiteatro. Constructed out of solid rock in the second century AD, it seated

Remains of the Roman amphitheatre in Cagliari

10,000 spectators (the city's entire population at the time). Although much of it has been destroyed, there is still a fascination in the former gladiatorial site.

5–6

Keep following the road down and turn left, remaining on Via Frà Ignazio da Laconi, to Ingresso No 11 for the **Orto Botánico** (Botanic Garden; ► 57). This pleasant, shady spot is the city's lungs.

6–7

On exit, turn left into Via Portoscalas past **Chiesa di San Michele**. Turn right onto Corso Vittorio Emanuele II, then right into Largo Carlo Felice and straight down to the **Via Roma**.

TAKING A BREAK

Il Caffè at 76 Largo Carlo Felice is a good place for a drink and a browse in their very good bookshop.

---

2 CAGLIARI TO VILLASIMÍUS

Drive

DISTANCE 51km (32mi) to Villasimíus (but with detours to beaches)
TIME 2–3 hours or a day with all detours **START POINT** Cagliari
Airport ✚ 176 A2 **END POINT** Villasimíus ✚ 177 D1

This drive takes you past the Golfo degli Ángeli (Bay of Angels) along the Strada Panorámica, which overlooks lovely beaches backed by low hills and covered with Mediterranean macchia. As you leave Cagliari behind, the coast becomes much quieter, the road twists and turns over hilly terrain with dramatic views of the sea, white sands and delightfully secluded coves begging to be explored.

1–2

Start from **Cagliari airport** (6km/3.5mi northwest of Cagliari centre) and going southeast take the SS554, following the signs for Quartu S Elena and Villasimíus (▶ 54). This is mainly dual carriageway around the ring road (and no tolls payable). As you get close to the sea, look out for flamingos in the lagoons left and right, Stagno Simbrizzi and Stagno di Quartu respectively. To reach **Poetto beach** (▶ 58) from here, turn west on the coast road past Spiaggia di Quartu and on to **Marina Piccola** (▶ 58) on Poetto beach.

1–2 (alternative)

If you're travelling from central Cagliari (▶ 50), follow Via Roma southeast, continuing straight at the end of the harbour on the street that becomes Viale Armando Diaz. Continue by turning on to

Ponto Vittorio and slightly left at Viale Poetto, then take a left turn at Via Lungo Saline.

Stop at the vast **Poetto beach** (▶ 55; it is more than 8km/5mi long) with its fine, white sand, and admire the lagoon of Molentargius behind it, which is frequented by flamingos and many other wetland birds.

2–3

Continue along the panoramic Cagliari to Villasimíus coastal road

to the locality of **Sant' Andrea** (on the left). For a detour to the beach turn right a little further along into Via Taormina, which brings you to the shore.

On the western side there are remains of a third century AD Roman villa and thermal baths to be seen.

3–4

Return to the scenic coast road and after just over 13km (8mi) you arrive at **Gereméas** with its long, white sandy beaches. Nearby, to the east, is **Torre delle Stelle** where you can take a dirt road east from the village centre to the beach. There are bars and shops by the white-golden sand and a lovely panorama.

4–5

On the coastal road follow the signs for **Solánas**, about 32km (20mi) from Cagliari. The main road loops around, giving access to the beach at the main car park in the centre, but choose the prettier, eastern side, remarkable for its dune at the base of **Capo Boi**. The large, golden sandy beach extends to the west of this promontory, overseen by a 16th-century watchtower, Torre di Capo Boi.

5–6

Continue back on the main road and after 11km (7mi) take the right turn going south signposted **Capo Carbonara**. This is the most south-easterly point of Sardinia and from here there are excellent views. Rejoin the main road, which brings you into **Villasimíus** (➤ 54).

TAKING A BREAK

Stop for lunch at **Ristorante da Barbara**, Strada Provinciale per Villasimíus, in Solánas (tel: 070 750 630), or sit down at **Bar Giò** on the Piazza Gramsci in Villasimíus and enjoy the colourful hustle and bustle from an ideal vantage point.

The rocky shoreline between Villasimíus and Cagliari

Walks & Tours

3 ORISTANO & PENISOLA DEL SINIS
Drive

DISTANCE 49km (30mi)
TIME Half a day
START/END POINT Oristano ⊞ 170 C2

This leisurely drive takes you to the seaside resort of Marina di Torre Grande and then through the "flamingo heaven" lagoon world of Místras and Cabras before reaching the tip of the Sinis Peninsula at the remains of the gloriously sited ancient city of Tharros.

1–2

Take the SS292 north from **Oristano** (➤ 74) following signs to Marina di Torre Grande and Cuglieri. A long bridge crosses the Tirso, after which you come to a fork in the road. Take the left fork, following signs for Cabras/Tharros and keep following signs for San Giovanni di Sinis. About 9km (5.5mi) outside Oristano you come to **Marina di Torre Grande** (➤ 78). This is a buzzing seaside resort (in season) with a long, sandy beach that shelves gently and has water sports.

2–3

Head back to the main road and at the intersection take the left-hand turn towards San Giovanni di Sinis. On both sides you now have lagoons. On your left is the Stagno di Místras, while on the right is the **Stagno di Cabras** (➤ 72), the largest in Italy at 2,000ha (5,000 acres). Besides flamingos, the lagoon also teems with fish, especially mullet, which is used to make the prized *bottarga* (mullet roe; ➤ 28). Go straight on, past a right turn towards Tharros, to **San Giovanni di Sinis**.

3–4

This sleepy fishing village's Chiesa di San Giovanni di Sinis is, after Cagliari's San Saturnino, the oldest church in Sardinia, dating from AD476. The interior is refreshingly bare and simple. Behind the church, near the sea, are some remaining thatched *domus de cruccuri* (rush huts) once used by fishermen. From San Giovanni di Sinis walk or take the little tourist train to the nearby entrance of the ancient town of Tharros.

4–5

Founded around 730BC, **Tharros** (➤ 73) was the most prosperous of the west coast Phoenician port cities. After the Roman conquest in 238BC, however, it gradually fell into disuse as trade shifted to Oristano in 1070. The archaeological site reveals mostly the Roman city, but there is still a temple with Doric half-columns and a children's burial ground *(tophet)* dating from

Corinthian columns, Tharros

View across the lagoon to the Sinis Peninsula

the Phoenician city. An old watchtower stands sentinel on the headland and the coast is fringed by lovely beaches, including the nearby beach of Is Arutas.

5–6

Return the same way until you reach the left turn to San Salvatore/Riola, 4km (2.5mi) north. Once the setting for spaghetti westerns, the dusty little town of **San Salvatore** (► 78) is hugely atmospheric, although often deserted except for the Barefoot Race in September.

6–7

Go northeast on SP7 towards SP59 for 7km (4.5mi) then turn right at the SS292 after 1km (0.6mi) and take the next right at Via Sant'Anna into Riola Sardo. Continue on the SS292 back to Oristano.

TAKING A BREAK

Have a drink in Marina di Torre Grande in one of the beach bars on the palm-lined esplanade.

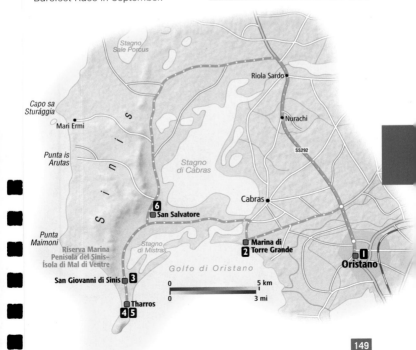

4 ALGHERO
Walk

DISTANCE 2km (1.2mi) **TIME** 2–3 hours	
START POINT Piazza Porta Terra ✚ 166 B2	
END POINT Piazza Civica ✚ 166 B2	

A café terrace in **Piazza Civica**

This walk takes you through the old town of Alghero (➤ 110), protected by ancient walls and towers. In the web of narrow streets you may pass washing hung beneath shuttered windows, and the city's most important churches and museums. The walk culminates in the main piazza, where Charles V addressed the crowds in 1541 before going off to fight the Turks.

❶–❷

Start at **Piazza Porta Terra** (➤ 110) opposite the top end of the Giardino Públbico. The Porta Terra was one of the walled town's two gates, and is now an interpretation centre; climb the 32 steps to the top for excellent views of the town. Coming out of here, turn left into Carrer de los Arjoles and then right into Via

Insider Tip

Statues in Chiesa di San Francesco

Ambrogion Machin. At the end of this road turn right into Via Carlo Alberto and you'll come to the **Chiesa di San Francesco** (➤ 110) on the right. This is one of Alghero's landmarks, with its stately, pointed Aragonese tower, and is an excellent example of Catalan architecture. Parts of the cloisters date back to the 13th century. Concerts are staged in this lovely setting during the summer.

❷–❸

From the church turn left and walk back down Via Carlo Alberto. This street is Alghero's main shopping hub, full of boutiques and jewellery shops brimming with coral. Continue straight on crossing over Via Gilbert Ferret. Known as the *"quatre contonades"* (four sides), this junction was where piecemeal labourers would, over the centuries,

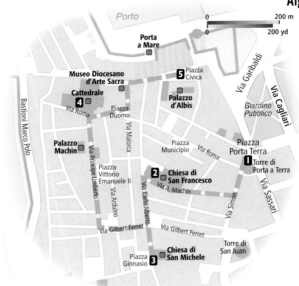

assemble in the hope of getting work.

After this, on the left-hand side, you come to the 17th-century **Chiesa di San Michele** (➤ 110). This opulent baroque church dominates the skyline with its glistening ceramic dome, and has fine altar paintings.

3–4

From San Michele walk back to Via Gilbert Ferret and turn left, then right into Via Principe Umberto, one of the old centre's most attractive lanes. The 17th-century **Palazzo Machin** (Nos 9–11) was built for a local bishop and, although now crumbling, it still has fine Catalan-Gothic windows.

Continue up the street and ahead of you, just to the right, is the cathedral's octagonal campanile. Walk around into Piazza Duomo and see the **Cattedrale di Santa Maria** (➤ 106).

Inside there is a jumble of styles and overblown baroque touches although some parts of the original 16th-century building still remain.

4–5

Go out of the Cattedrale and head next door to the **Museo Diocesano d'Arte Sacra**, housed in the former Rosario church. This is the perfect setting for an array of priceless religious art. Walk east past Via Maiorca, Via Carlo Alberto and Vicolo Sena to arrive at **Piazza Civica**, the old town's main square, known as *il salotto* (the dining room). It is just inside **Port a Mare** (Sea Gate) and is full of outdoor bars and parasols. On the opposite side of the piazza is the Gothic **Palazzo d'Albis**, from where Charles V told the assembled throng, *"Estade todos caballeros"* ("You are all knights").

TAKING A BREAK

You must do the short walk on the *bastione*, the town wall between the harbour and the Piazza Sulis. Several bars along the wall entice guests to go in and enjoy the fantastic view over Capo Cáccia. It is the place to meet at sunset!

Insider Tip

5 GENNARGENTU MOUNTAINS
Drive

DISTANCE 77km (48mi)
TIME Half-day to full day
START/END POINT Núoro ✚ 172 C4

This scenic drive takes you through granite-strewn rolling countryside framed by lush vegetation of Mediterranean *macchia*, cork, holm and oak trees. There are tracks and gorges and majestic mountains, and the famous Nepente vineyards around Oliena that produce some of the island's finest Cannonau.

1–2

Leave **Núoro** (➤ 94) heading east on the Via Trieste. Continue on this road, which becomes the Via Ballero, then turn left at Viale La Solitudine. After 300m bear slightly right onto the SP42, Via Monte Ortobene. Continue along this panoramic road as it twists upwards. (From Núoro the journey is about 8km/5mi.) You will come to some speed humps on the road followed by souvenir stalls and a couple of bars/restaurants. Leave your car in the car park near the top of **Monte Ortobene** (➤ 96) and follow the faded yellow sign saying *"Il Redentore"*. A walk of around 100m along a dusty track brings you to 49 rock steps up to the bronze sculpture of *Christ the Redeemer* (➤ 96).

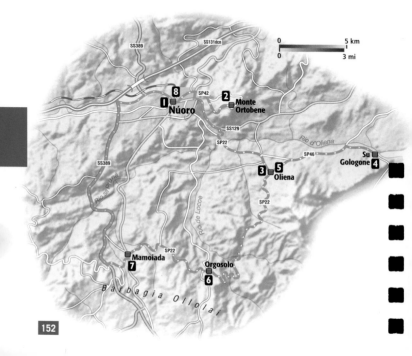

The scenery along the Núoro to Monte Ortobene road

2–3

The next stage, **Oliena** (➤96), is 12km (7.5mi) away. Leave Monte Ortobene heading northwest on the SP42 towards the SP45/Via Valverde. Bear slightly left at SP45/Viale La Solitudine and turn left at SP45. Take a sharp left at the SS129. After 4.3km (2.7mi) turn right at the SP22 and continue on the SP22 by turning left. Bear slightly right at Via Raffaele Calamida then turn right at Via Núoro/SP46 and follow tourist information signs to the main Via Deledda. Here is a good place to pick up information on the area and excursions (including Tiscali ➤92 and **Gola Su Gorruppu** ➤98). Oliena is a very pretty town full of whitewashed houses with balconies, terraces and strange chimneypots. Perhaps taking a cue from neighbouring Orgosolo, Oliena has several wall murals, and in the parish church a Christmas *presepio* (nativity scene) by a local artist. Produced here are the excellent, fruity Cannonau wines as well as filigree silver and gold jewellery and delicately embroidered silk shawls.

3–4

A little diversion 6km (3.5mi) east on the Dorgali road/SP46 takes you to **Su Gologone**, named after its spring, which rises close to the church of San Giovanni. It is also a good spot for embarking on expeditions to Tiscali and/or Gola Su Gorruppu but note that these would take up to around four hours and involve some arduous trekking. The legendary hotel Su Gologone (➤99) located near the source is a popular starting and finishing point for organised excursions to the Supramonte mountains.

4–5

Retrace your steps on the SP46 to Oliena.

5–6

After about 7km (4.5mi) outside Oliena turn left at the SP58 and follow this twisting, scenic road for about 11km (7mi) until you see

The lush countryside near Oliena

the entrance to **Orgosolo** (➤ 97).
Known as the "capital of the
Barbagia" and former refuge of
the area's most notorious bandits,
it is also famous for the murals that
cover every available space depicting political themes and the locals'
struggle to maintain their culture.

6–7

From Orgosolo head west for 10km
(6mi) to **Mamoiada** (➤ 97). Take
the SP22/Corso Republica towards
Via di Vittorio and continue on the
SP22. Famous for its masked
festivals (➤ 16), especially at
Carnival time in February/March,
Mamoiada's Museo delle Maschere

TAKING A BREAK

The spring is a lovely place for a picnic,
or you can also head for the charming
bar of the **Su Gologone restaurant/hotel**
(➤ 99). The restaurant serves top
traditional Sardinian cuisine.

Mediterranee (➤ 97) shows the
famous *mamuthones* and
issohadores costumed figures.

7–8

From Mamoiada head southwest
on Via Matteotti towards Via Núoro
and turn right, then bear slightly
right again at SS389/Via Vittorio
Emanuele II and follow the SS389
to Núoro (16km/10mi).

6 ÍSOLA CAPRERA
Walk

DISTANCE 12.5km (8mi) **TIME** 4 hours
START/END POINT Car park, Caprera (350m after the causeway from
La Maddalena) ✚ 169 D4

This walk takes you through the
archipelago's greenest island,
known also as "Garibaldi's island".
Giuseppe Garibaldi loved La
Caprera's freedom and peace so
much that he chose to spend the
last 27 years of his life here
(➤ 136). Stroll through *macchia*
and past green pines enjoying
stunning views over the surrounding
islands and across to Corsica. The
island's highest peak, pink granite
Monte Telaione, reaches up to
212m (695ft), where you may see
peregrine falcons. You could also
choose to take a detour to the lovely
Cala Coticcio (also called Cala
Tahiti) beach.

1–2

From the car park, take the footpath that forks right into the
macchia going south. Follow this
main path through the scented

The views from Ísola Caprera are idyllic

myrtle, juniper, lentisk, lavender
and wild flowers, ignoring the
short tracks down to the coast.
After about 15 minutes
you come to a grove of
umbrella pine trees.
Turn right at the next
fork and on your
right is the Cala
Stagnali – a little
cove with coarse
sand. Keep straight
on the main track
to an asphalt road
onto which you bear
right. At the fork turn
left and begin the
ascent looking out over

**Parco Nazionale dell'
Arcipélago La Maddalena**

Ísola Budelli
Ísola Maddalena
Ísola Spargi
La Maddalena
Museo Garibaldino
Stagnali •
Ísola Caprera
Palau
Capannaccia
Punta Rossa
SS133

0   5 ʰ
0   3 ⁿ

A blissfully quiet road on Ísola Caprera

Continue along this road to a lay-by on the left, then after 50m take a little detour by turning sharp right and climb up the steps to **Monte Teliaone** – Caprera's highest peak – with its lookout tower.

3–4

Return to the road and turn right to continue. After about 3 hours (in total), shortly after you pass a derelict house on the left, follow the road as it bears left and the asphalted road runs out. On reaching a track junction, turn down to the left. (The track straight ahead leads to Monte Arbuticci's gun emplacement.) Ignore the two turns on your right and go straight ahead.

4–5

At a junction go left past two Military Zone buildings on the right and up to a reservoir (about 3.5 hours). Cross the wall of the dam, following the ascending path, which eventually flattens out leading to a car park. Follow the granite drive on the right past wind-sculpted granite rocks to the **Compendio Garibaldino di Caprera** (► 136).

5–6

Before the Garibaldi buildings, take the short concrete drive on the left to a little terrace. Carry on downhill on the path below the enclosed estate until the path descends between rocks. At a small house bear right before joining a road that takes you past houses. Follow the main road left back to the small car park.

the archipelago's islands and Corsica. After about an hour and a quarter of walking, you'll see the peak of **Poggio Rasu** (Bare Hill) on your right. The road bends to the left but carry straight along the track to the World War II gun emplacement built from granite.

2–3

Return to the bend and continue right, ascending along the road. After a short distance the road begins to level out and descend. At a T-junction turn right past a derelict fountain on the left and a concrete building on the right.

> **TAKING A BREAK**
>
> The **I Mille** is a simple kiosk with tables and benches, idyllically located in a pine wood by the road. A small oasis in which you can buy excellent *paninis* and other snacks.

Practicalities

Practicalities

BEFORE YOU GO

WHAT YOU NEED

		UK	USA	Canada	Australia	Ireland	Netherlands
● Required ○ Suggested ▲ Not required △ Not applicable	Some countries require a passport to remain valid for a minimum period (usually at least 6 months) beyond the date of entry – check before you travel.						
Passport/National Identity Card		●	●	●	●	●	●
Visa (for less than three months)		▲	▲	▲	▲	▲	▲
Onward or Return Ticket		▲	●	●	●	▲	▲
Health Inoculations (tetanus and polio)		▲	▲	▲	▲	▲	▲
Travel Insurance		○	○	○	○	○	○
Driving Licence (national) for car rental		●	●	●	●	●	●
Car Insurance Certificate (if using own car)		●	△	△	△	●	●
Car Registration Document (if using own car)		●	△	△	△	●	●

WHEN TO GO

Cagliari

High season   Low season

JAN	FEB	MAR	APR	MAY	JUN	JUL	AUG	SEP	OCT	NOV	DEC
10°C	11°C	13°C	19°C	22°C	25°C	31°C	31°C	26°C	22°C	16°C	12°C
50°F	53°F	55°F	66°F	72°F	75°F	88°F	88°F	29°F	72°F	61°F	54°F

☀ Sun   ⛅ Sunshine and showers   🌧 Wet   🌧 Very wet

Sardinia has a very **pleasant six-month summer**, usually hot and dry from May to October but cooled by a breeze as it is the middle of the Mediterranean. In March and April evenings can be cool, but this is a **good time for walking**, when the island is covered in flowers, and there are also a number of excellent festivals. From May onwards it is usually warm enough for swimming. July and August are the **peak season** and are often swelteringly hot as well as extremely busy. September can also be very hot, but it is much less crowded. Autumn sees a second flowering of plants, while in the winter the weather can still be warm and clear with **snowfalls** in the interior, where it is possible to ski. Note that many hotels and restaurants around the coast are only open from May to September. The above temperatures are the maximum daily average.

ITALIAN STATE TOURIST BOARD (ENIT): www.enit.it; www.italiantourism.com

In Italy
Via Parigi 11, 00185 Rome
☎ 06 488 991
www.enit.it

In the UK
1 Princes Street
London W1B 2AY
☎ 020 7408 1254
www.enit.it

In the US
630 Fifth Avenue
Suite 1565, New York, NY 10111
☎ 212/245-5618
www.italiantourism.com

GETTING THERE

BY AIR Sardinia is served by three airports: Alghero in the northwest, Ólbia in the northeast and Cagliari in the south. **From the UK** From London airports, easyJet (www.easyjet.com) flies to Cagliari and Ólbia, and Ryanair (www.ryanair.com) flies to Alghero and Cagliari. Other scheduled airlines operate in the summer such as BMI and British Airways, and there are many regional flights too. The flight time is 2–3 hours. **From the US and Canada** There are no direct flights to the island, but there are flights to the mainland from several cities. The main hubs are Milan and Rome, from where there are plenty of connecting flights. The national airline, Alitalia, has the widest selection of routes between the US and Italy. Flying time to the mainland is 8–10 hours from the east coast and around 11 hours from the west coast. Connections to Sardinia take another hour or two. The most frequent flights are between Rome and Cagliari. **From Australia and New Zealand** There are no direct flights but Air New Zealand and Qantas fly to Milan and Rome, from where it is easy to pick up a connecting flight. You could also fly to the UK first and then pick up a flight as there are so many options. Flying time to mainland Italy from Australia's east coast is 21 hours and from New Zealand is 24 hours.

BY SEA There are several options to cross the English Channel to France and many routes from France and Italy to Sardinia: Marseille to Porto Tórres (northwest coast), Rome (Civitavecchia) to Golfo Aranci or Ólbia (northeast coast) and Genova to Porto Tórres or Ólbia, for example. There are also fast ferries from Nice to Bastia in Corsica and daily ferries from Bonifacio to Santa Teresa on the northern tip of Sardinia. The most important shipping companies in Sardinia are Moby Lines (www.mobylines.com), Sardinia Ferries (www.corsica-ferries.co.uk) and Grandi Navi Veloci (www.gnv.it). The former municipal service Tirrenia is now owned by the CIN consortium, of which Moby Lines holds a significant percentage. At the time information was being collected for this publication, there were plans to reduce the prices that had risen considerably due to the market concentration by introducing an inexpensive "Flotta Sarda".

TIME

 Like mainland Italy, Sardinia is one hour ahead of GMT, although daylight saving applies from April to October, making it GMT +2.

CURRENCY & FOREIGN EXCHANGE

Currency The legal currency of Sardinia is the euro (€), which is split into 100 cents (*centésimi*). Euro notes are issued in denominations of 5, 10, 20, 50, 100, 200 and 500. There are eight different coin denominations – 1 and 2 euros, then 50, 20, 10, 5, 2 and 1 cents. **Exchange** Cash and most major travellers' cheques can be exchanged at banks and at kiosks *(cambio)* at the airports and large hotels. **Credit and debit cards** Credit cards are widely accepted, except in B&Bs and *agriturismi*, but many smaller establishments prefer cash. Most towns have a bank with an ATM where you can use a credit or debit card, although using the former is usually expensive.

In Australia
Level 4, 46 Market Street
Sydney, NSW 2000
☎ 02 9262 1666
www.enit.it

In Canada
175 Bloor St East
Suite 907, South Tower
Toronto, ON, M4W 3R8
☎ 416/925 4882

WEBSITES

- www.regione.sardegna.it
- www.sardegnaturismo.it
- www.sardegna-digitallibrary.it
- www.sardegnaturismo.it
- www.holidays-in-sardinia.com
- www.sarnow.com

Practicalities

WHEN YOU ARE THERE

NATIONAL HOLIDAYS

1 Jan	New Year's Day
6 Jan	Epiphany
March/April	Good Friday and Easter Monday
25 April	Liberation Day
1 May	Labour Day
2 June	Republic Day
15 Aug	Ferragosto (Assumption)
1 Nov	Ognissanti (All Saints)
8 Dec	Immaculate Conception
25 Dec	Christmas Day
26 Dec	St Stephen's Day

ELECTRICITY

 The current is 220 volts AC. However, appliances requiring 240 volts AC also work. Plugs are standard two-round-pin continental types. UK, North American and Australasian visitors will need an adaptor, and US visitors will need a voltage transformer.

OPENING HOURS

○ Shops
● Offices
● Banks
● Main Post Offices
● Museums/Monuments
● Pharmacies

8am 9am 10am noon 1pm 2pm 16pm 5pm 7pm

☐ Day ☐ Midday ☐ Evening

Some close Monday morning and most shops are closed on Sunday. **Museum** times vary but are usually daily 9–1, 4–8 (3–7 in winter). Some museums close on Monday. Archaeological sites usually open from 9 to one hour before sunset. Smaller museums and places of interest have limited opening during winter and some close down completely.

TIPS/GRATUITIES

Small tips are often expected. As a general guide:

Restaurants (service included)	Change
Restaurants (service not included)	10%
Cafés/bars (if service not included)	Change/10%
Taxis and tour guides	Discretionary
Porters	€1–€2
Chambermaids	Discretionary
Hairdressers	10%
Toilets	Discretionary

KNOCK-OFF NO-NO

No matter how cute that Louis Vuitton knock-off may be, resist the temptation to buy it, especially from beach vendors. Italian police have begun a crackdown on illegally "branded" goods, fining the buyers a high fine.

TIME DIFFERENCES

Sardinia (CET)	London (GMT)	New York (EST)	Los Angeles (PST)	Sydney (AEST)
12 noon	← 11 noon	← 6am	← 3am	→ 9pm

STAYING IN TOUCH

Post The postal service is very slow. You can buy stamps *(francobolli)* at post offices, tobacconists *(tabacchi)* and some souvenir shops. Post offices are normally open Mon–Fri 8:10–6:50, Sat 8–1:15.

Public telephones Telecom Italia (TI) payphones can be found on streets and in bars and some restaurants. Usually you need a phone card *(scheda telefónica)*, available €3, €5 or €10 denominations and sold at newsstands or *tabacchi*. Tear the perforated

corner off before use. Phone tariffs are very expensive – among the highest in Europe. To get through to an English-speaking operator, dial 170.

International Dialling Codes
Dial 00 followed by

UK:	44	Irish Republic:	353
USA / Canada:	1	Australia:	61

Mobile providers and services Signals are quite good in most places. Be sure your provider allows you roving access to other networks. Mobiles work on the GSM European standard; visitors from North America can buy compatible SIM cards at phone and electronics shops in Cagliari and larger cities. Check your own provider's rates before travelling; it may be cheaper to make international or other calls from a land line.

WiFi and Internet Many hotels offer some type of Internet. Larger ones have WiFi in rooms and most provide it in at least some public area. There is often a charge (about €10 for 24 hours) for in-room use. Signal strength and connection speed varies greatly and you may need to take your laptop to the lobby even if there is supposedly in-room connectivity. WiFi is available in many cafés and most towns have an internet point; ask at the tourist office.

PERSONAL SAFETY

The bandits that once roved the mountains are long gone, and Sardinia is one of Italy's safest regions. However, in larger cities such as Cagliari it makes sense to take the usual precautions – petty theft related to drug addiction is on the increase.
To be safe:

■ Close bags and wear them in front, across your body.

■ Leave valuables and jewellery in the hotel safe.

■ Never leave luggage or other possessions visible in parked cars.

■ Wear your camera and don't leave it unattended in cafés and restaurants.

■ During the holiday season take particular care to lock up well when your car is going to be left unsupervised for a longer period, e.g. at the airport, beach car park and popular excursion points.

■ Because beaches are crowded in summer, they are especially tempting places for petty thieves (who are very likely not locals themselves). Don't leave anything on a lounger or towel that you can't afford to lose – especially your mobile.

Police assistance:
☎ 112 from any phone

POLICE	112
FIRE	115 (or 113)
AMBULANCE	118 (or 113)
GENERAL EMERGENCY	112 (or 113)

Practicalities

HEALTH

 Insurance You should always take out full travel insurance cover when visiting Sardinia. EU citizens can reclaim medical expenses if they travel with their European Health Insurance Card (EHIC). There are reciprocal arrangements between the Australian Medicare system and Italy, but comprehensive insurance is still advised.

 Doctors and Dentists Ask at a pharmacy or your hotel for details of English-speaking doctors. Common ailments include dehydration, sunburn, stomach upsets and mosquito bites. Use insect repellent and sun protection. Dental treatment is not covered by the health service and can be expensive – another reason to carry medical insurance.

 Weather The sun is at its hottest in July and August, with temperatures frequently over 40°C (104°F), but it's always possible to cool off in the sea or mountains. Two summer winds sweep across the island – the *maestrale* (mistral) from the northwest, and the sultry, sand-bearing sirocco from the south. You should take a sun hat, high-factor sun cream and plenty of water to drink.

 Medication Prescriptions and other medicines are available from pharmacies *(farmacie)*, indicated by a large green cross.

 Safe Water Tap water is generally safe to drink. During the summer, some of the coastal region put more chlorine in the water, so buy the *"Aqua Minerale Naturale"* for mixing baby food. Sardinia has many mountain springs from which you can drink. *"Acqua non potabile"* indicates non-drinking water.

CONCESSIONS

In practically all of the institutions, there is a substantial discount on the amount charged to those under 18 and to pensioners over 61 (generally 50%); not infrequently admission is even free of charge.

TRAVELLING WITH A DISABILITY

The national museums in Cagliari have dedicated ramps, lifts and lavatories, but otherwise wheelchair access is extremely limited. This is also true of medieval city centres, which often have cobbled streets. Top hotels are generally well equipped.

CHILDREN

Children are welcomed with open arms in Sardinia. The sun can be fierce so it is essential to provide adequate protection against sunburn and dehydration. Special attractions for children are marked out in this book with the logo shown above.

RESTROOMS

There are few public toilets on the island. Most bars have them (*bagno, gabinetto* or *toilette*), although it's always a good idea to carry some toilet tissue with you.

CUSTOMS

The import of wildlife souvenirs from rare or endangered species may be illegal or require a permit. Before buying, check your home country's regulations.

EMBASSIES & HIGH COMMISSIONS

UK (Cagliari)
☎ 070 82 86 28
www.gov.uk

USA (Rome)
☎ 06 4 67 41
italy.usembassy.gov

Ireland (Rome)
☎ 06 5 85 23 81
www.dfa.ie/irish-embassy/italy

Australia (Rome)
☎ 06 85 27 21
www.italy.embassy.gov.au

Canada (Rome)
☎ 06 85 44 41
Italy.gc.ca

Useful Words and Phrases

ITALIAN AND SARDO

The official language of Sardinia is **Italian**, and most Sardinians speak it clearly. The **Sardinian language** is a melting pot of many influences – around Alghero you will hear Catalan, for example – but if there is one language from which **Sard** takes its root it is Latin, and it is closer to this mother tongue than mainland Italian is; for example, Sard for house is *domus* rather than Italian *casa*. The other major difference is the replacement of the Italian definite articles *il*, *la*, *i* and *le* with *su*, *sa*, *sus*, *sos* and *sas*, similar to Catalan.

People appreciate you greeting them with a *buon giorno* or *buona sera*. *Grazie* (thank you) should be acknowledged with *Prego* (You're welcome). *Permesso?* (May I?) is the polite way of making your way through a crowded street.

SURVIVAL PHRASES

yes/no **si/non**
please **per favore**
Thank you **Grazie**
You're welcome **Di niente/Prego**
I'm sorry **Mi dispiace**
Goodbye **Arrivederci**
Good morning **Buongiorno**
Goodnight **Buona sera**
How are you? **Come sta?**
How much? **Quanto costa?**
I would like... **Vorrei...**
Open **Aperto**
Closed **Chiuso**
Today **Oggi**
Tomorrow **Domani**
Monday **Lunedì**
Tuesday **Martedì**
Wednesday **Mercoledì**
Thursday **Giovedì**
Friday **Venerdì**
Saturday **Sabato**
Sunday **Domenica**

DIRECTIONS

I'm lost **Mi sono perso/a**
Where is...? **Dove si trova...?**
the station **la stazione**
the telephone **il telefono**
the bank **la banca**
the toilet **il gabinetto**
Turn left **Volti a sinistra**
Turn right **Volti a destra**
Go straight on **Vada dritto**
At the corner **all'angolo**
the street **la strada**
the building **il palazzo**
the traffic light **il semaforo**
the crossroads **l'incrocio**
the signs for... **le indicazione per...**

IF YOU NEED HELP

Help! **Aiuto!**
Could you help me, please?
   Mi potrebbe aiutare?
Do you speak English?
   Parla inglese?
I don't understand
   Non capisco
Please could you call a doctor quickly?
   Mi chiami presto un medico,
   per favore

ACCOMMODATION

Do you have a single/double room?
   Ha una camera singola/doppia?
with/without bath/toilet/shower
   con/senza vasca/gabinetto/doccia
Does that include breakfast?
   E'inclusa la prima colazione?
Does that include dinner?
   E'inclusa la cena?
Do you have room service?
   C'è il servizio in camera?
Could I see the room?
   E'possibile vedere la camera?

RESTAURANT

I'd like to book a table
   Vorrei prenotare un tavolo
A table for two, please
   Un tavolo per due, per favore
Could we see the menu, please?
   Ci porta la lista, per favore?
What's this?
   Cosa è questo?
A bottle of/a glass of...
   Una bottiglia di/un bicchiere di...
Could I have the bill?
   Ci porta il conto

Useful Words and Phrases

MENU READER

Sardinian specialities:
bottargo mullet roe
bue rosso prized Sardinian beef
cavallo horse
cordula lamb tripe
culurgiones ravioli filled with potato and cheese
mallareddus small pasta
porceddu roast suckling pig
sebada baked pastry filled with cheese and honey
suspiros sweets made with almonds, eggs and lemon
zuppa Gallura hearty baked dish of bread, cheese and broth
zurrette black pudding

Other menu items:
acciuga anchovy
acqua water
affettati sliced cured meats
affumicato smoked
aglio garlic
agnello lamb
anatra duck
antipasti hors d'oeuvres
arista roast pork
arrosto roast
asparagi asparagus
birra beer
bistecca steak
bollito boiled meat
braciola minute steak
brasato braised
brodo broth
budino pudding

burro butter
cacciagione game
cacciatore, alla rich tomato sauce with mushrooms
caffè corretto/macchiato coffee with liqueur/spirit, or with a drop of milk
caffè freddo iced coffee
caffè latte milky coffee
caffè lungo weak coffee
caffè ristretto strong coffee
calamaro squid
cappero caper
carciofo artichoke
carne meat
carota carrot
carpa carp
casalingo home-made
cavolfiore cauliflower
cavolo cabbage
ceci chickpeas
cervello brains
cervo venison
cetriolino gherkin
cetriolo cucumber
cicoria chicory
cinghiale boar
cioccolata chocolate
cipolla onion
coda di bue oxtail
coniglio rabbit
contorni vegetables
coperto cover charge
coscia leg of meat
cotolette cutlets
cozze mussels
crema custard
crudo raw
dolci cakes/desserts

erbe aromatiche herbs
facito stuffed
fagioli beans
fagiolini green beans
fegato liver
finocchio fennel
formaggio cheese
forno, al baked
frittata omelette
fritto fried
frizzante fizzy
frulatto whisked
frutti di mare seafood
funghi mushrooms
gamberetto shrimp
gelato icecream
ghiaccio ice
gnocchi potato dumplings
granchio crab
gran(o)turco corn
griglia, alla grilled
imbottito stuffed
insalata salad
IVA VAT
latte milk
lepre hare
lumache snails
manzo beef
merluzzo cod
miele honey
minestra soup
molluschi shellfish
olio oil
oliva olive
ostrica oyster
pancetta bacon
pane bread
panino roll
panna cream
pastasciutta dried pasta with sauce
pasta sfoglia puffpastry
patate fritte chips
pecora mutton
pecorino sheep'smilk cheese

peperone red/green pepper
pesce fish
petto breast
piccione pigeon
piselli peas
pollame fowl
pollo chicken
polpetta meatball
prezzemolo parsley
primo piatto first course
ragù meat sauce
ripieno stuffed
riso rice
salsiccia sausage
saltimbocca veal with prosciutto and sage
secco dry
secondo piatto main course
senape mustard
servizio compreso service included
sogliola sole
succa di frutta fruit juice
sugo sauce
tonno tuna
uovo affrogato/in carnica poached egg
uovo al tegamo/fritto fried egg
uovo alla coque soft boiled egg
uovo alla sodo hard boiled egg
uova strapazzate scambled egg
verdure vegetables
vino wine
bianco white
rosato rosé
rosso red
vitello veal
zucchero sugar
zucchino courgette
zuppa soup

Road Atlas

For chapters: See inside front cover

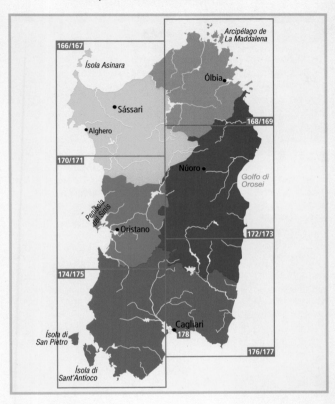

Key to Road Atlas

A 18 Motorway	
Dual carriageway	
SS114 Trunk road	
Main road	
Secondary road	
Road under construction/planned	
Railway	
Ferry route	
International boundary	
Province boundary	
National park, National preserve	
Restricted area	

✈ ✈	(International) airport
⛪ ⛪	Monastery / Church, chapel
♟ ♟	Castle, fortress / Ruin
★ ∴	Place of interest / Archaeological site
⛋ ⛯	Tower / Lighthouse
∭ ∩	Waterfall / Cave
⛨ ⌂	Nuraghe / Dolmen
⛐ ⚓	Radio mast / (Swimming) beach
⚲ ⚓	Spa / yacht harbour
★	TOP 10
26	Don't Miss
22	At Your Leisure

1 : 440 000

0	10	20 km

0	5	10 mi

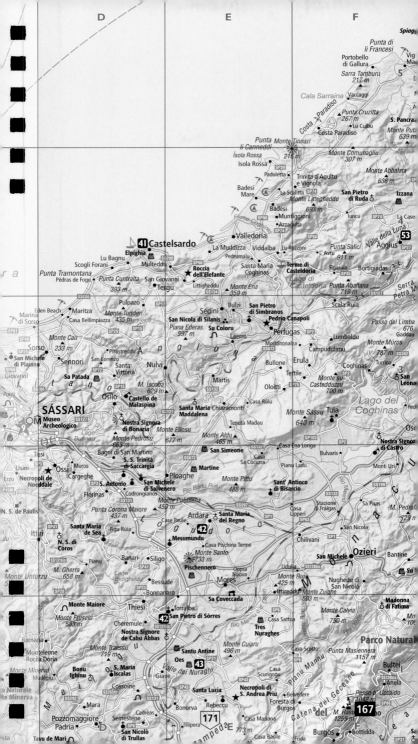

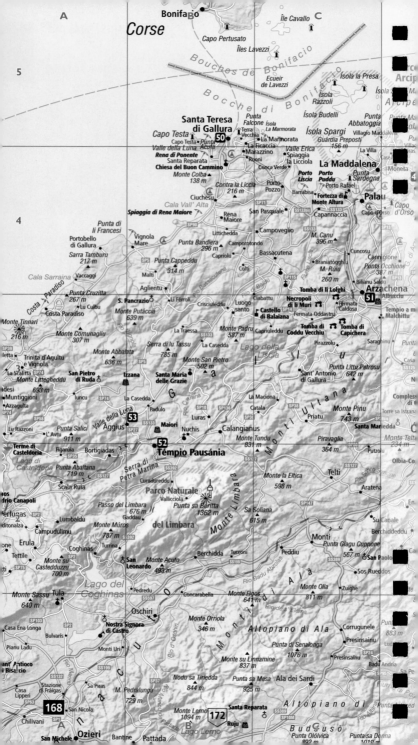

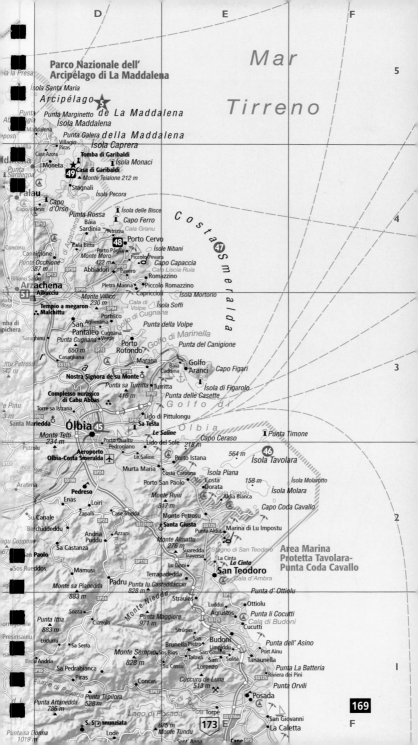

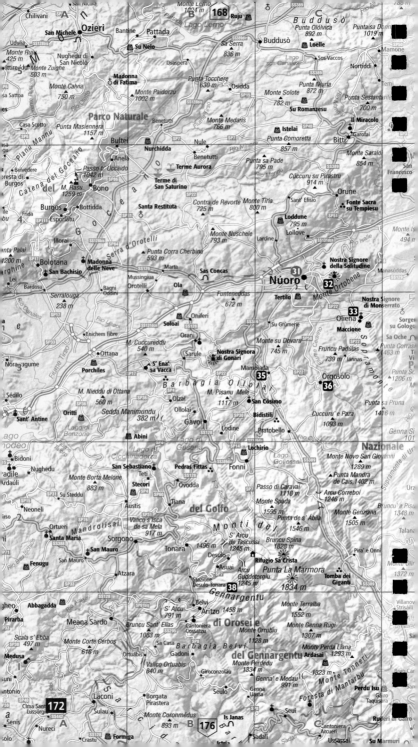

555 m
Parco Atzei
Funtanazza
Cala Campu Sali
Marina di Arbus
Monte Arcuentu
785 m
Fortezza
Portu Maga
SP65
Punta Nuracciolu
938 m
Villagio
Rigu
Piscinas
Montevecchio
Miniera
Montevecchio
19
Ingurtosu-Gennamari
Ingurtosu
Arbus
Punta su Pinnori
273 m
Naracauli
A
Bau
r
b
Casa Atzeni
Gennamari
Passo Bidderdi
492 m
Casa Marigosa

Punta Mumullonis
499 m
Monte Lina
Capo Pecora
Rio Mannu
Punta Mairu
724 m
Portixeddu
Fluminimaggiore
Parco Naturale
San Nicolao
Monte M
1021
Buggerru
Serra Tirus
693 m
Su Mannau
Tempio di Antas
de
Linas
Margan
Planu Sartu
Malfidano
Arenas
Cala Domestica
Gruqua
Sant'
Angelo
Sa Duchessa
Acquaresi
Arcu Genna
Bogai 549 m
Malacalzetta
SS126
San Benedetto
Monte Guardianu
537 m
Montecani
Perdu Carta
Masua
Case Lenzu
Pan di Zucchero
Porto Flavia
Cala
Fontanesus
San Gio
Don
Nebida
Punta San Michele
906 m
Golfo di
Iglesias
Agruxiau
SP64
Monteponi
SS130
Monte Scorca
Binous
Fontanamare
San Giovanni
Gonnesa
Séddas Modizzis
Tonnara
Gonnesa 455 m
Rio Cixerri
Villan
Seruci
Barega
Monte Exi
369 m
Seruci
Bacu Abis
Capo Altano o Giordano
Ísola del Meli
Piolanas
Monte San Mai
614 m
Nuraxi Figus
Cortoghiana
Terraseo
Portopaglietto
Medau Desogus
Portovesme
Punta Brabion
407 m
Portoscuso
Santa Maria di
Flumentepido
Barbusi
Sirri
Narcac
La Punta
Ísola Piana
Parco Archeologico
di Monte Sirai
Punta delle Oche
Tonnare
Sirai
Guardia dei Mori
221 m
Tacca Rossa
Paringianu
Carbonaxia
Carbonia
Pesus
Cala Fico
Is Fonnesus
Necropoli
Capo Sandalo
Carloforte
Punta s' Aliga
Bruncuteula
Perdaxius
Montesso
Ísola del Corno
Peschiera di
Ba Cerbus
Is Pitus
20
Becca Tomaso
162 m
Ísola di
Matzaccara
Monte San Giovanni
332 m
Lago di
San Pietro
La Caletta
Is Urigus
Monte Pranu
Cala dello
La Bobba
San Giovanni
Suergiu
Santa
Maria
Fo
Spalmatore
Calasetta
Pian
Salina
Tratalias
Giba
Punta delle
Colonne
Cussorgia
Is Loddis
Palmas
Piscir
Punta
Maggiore
Antica Locan
Tonnara
SS195
Stagno di
Santa Caterina
Is Pistis
Villario
Rosella
Sant'Antioco
Cortias
Saline
Is F
Ponti
Punta de
s' Aliga
Porto Botte
Stagno di
Porto Botte
Punta Caragoli
Mercuri
Perdas de Fogu
271 m
Santa
Maria
Is Solinas
Barussa
Cala Lunga
Ciclopi
Spiaggia
Canisoni
Golfo
Stagno di
Is Spigas
Cala de Saboni
Tonnara
Maladroxia
di Palmas
Maestrale
Is Pilloni
21
Ísola di Sant'Antioco
Cannai
Cala su Turcu
Porto Pino
Monte Arbus 239 m
Porto Sciusciau
Torre Cannai
Punta Menga
Stagno de
is Bre
Capo Sperone
La Fazenda
Ísola la Vacca
Porto
Pino
Porto Zaffaraneddu
Monte Lapanu
311 m
Don Antioco
Punta di Cala Piombo
Cala Piombo
Porto d
Punta de
228

Ísola il Toro

Cagliari

178

Index

Index

Index

Index / Picture Credits

Picture Credits

Credits

1st Edition 2017

Worldwide Distribution: Marco Polo Travel Publishing Ltd
Pinewood, Chineham Business Park
Crockford Lane, Chineham
Basingstoke, Hampshire RG24 8AL, United Kingdom.
© MAIRDUMONT GmbH & Co. KG, Ostfildern

Authors: Adele Evans, Peter Höh
Editor: Isolde Bacher, textdienst
Translation and revised editing: Sarah Trenker, Munich
Program supervisor: Birgit Borowski
Chief editor: Rainer Eisenschmid

Cartography: © MAIRDUMONT GmbH & Co. KG, Ostfildern
3D-illustrations: jangled nerves, Stuttgart

Printed in China

Despite all of our authors' thorough research, errors can creep in. The publishers do not accept any liability for this. Whether you want to praise us, alert us to errors or give us a personal tip – please don't hesitate to email or post to:

MARCO POLO Travel Publishing Ltd
Pinewood, Chineham Business Park
Crockford Lane, Chineham
Basingstoke, Hampshire RG24 8AL
United Kingdom
Email: sales@marcopolouk.com

FSC
www.fsc.org
MIX
Paper from
responsible sources
FSC® C124385

10 REASONS
TO COME BACK AGAIN

1. The **anticipation** when entering the harbour will get you hooked for life!

2. Sardinia's coastline is so diverse that you will find a new **dream beach every time you go there**.

3. The unobtrusive **friendliness** and helpfulness of the Sards has a magical charm.

4. You need time to enjoy the many **delicacies and specialities** of the island!

5. The excursion to the spectacular cliffs of the **Gulf of Orosei** takes your breath away every time.

6. Sardinia's **unspoilt, tranquil mountain region** relaxes you in an enchanting way.

7. The isolated coasts of the island are a constant invitation to go for **walks along the beaches.**

8. In the **lively capital of** Cagliari, you will want time to soak up the atmosphere.

9. **Sunsets** on the bastion of Alghero are all – in their own way – somehow unique.

10. Once you have heard it once, **the sound of the shepherds' flutes** fills every heart with longing.